Jeremiah

Daring to Hope in an Unstable World

A Bible Study by

Melissa Spoelstra

Abingdon Press
Nashville

JEREMIAH: DARING TO HOPE IN AN UNSTABLE WORLD

This book is printed on acid-free paper.

ISBN 978-1-4267-8887-1

20 21 22 23 — 19 18 17 16

MANUFACTURED IN THE UNITED STATES OF AMERICA

Contents

About the Author

Melissa Spoelstra is a popular women's conference speaker, Bible teacher, and writer who is madly in love with Jesus and passionate about studying God's Word and helping women of all ages to seek Christ and know Him more intimately through serious Bible study. Having a degree in Bible theology, she enjoys teaching God's Word to the body of Christ, traveling to diverse groups and churches across the nation and recently to Nairobi, Kenya, for a women's prayer conference. Melissa has published articles in *ParentLife*, *Women's Spectrum*, and *Just Between Us* and writes a regular blog in which she shares her musings about what God is teaching her on any given day. She lives in Dublin, Ohio, with her pastor husband, Sean, and their four kids: Zach, Abby, Sara, and Rachel.

Follow Melissa:

Twitter	@MelSpoelstra
Instagram	@Daring2Hope
Facebook	@AuthorMelissaSpoelstra
Her blog	MelissaSpoelstra.com (check here also for event dates and booking information)

Introduction

When we look around at today's world, *hope* usually isn't the first word that comes to mind. In many ways we live in an age of uncertainty. If we allow our thoughts to linger on things such as the national debt, the pesticide-covered food supply, the condition of the environment, the increase in violence toward even our most innocent, and the looming moral bankruptcy of our culture, we can get pretty discouraged. The situation only compounds when we add our personal issues to these corporate ones. Life can be rough. When marriages fail, bank accounts run low, friendships end, or the everyday demands of a fast-paced life get us down, we sometimes feel the ground shaking beneath our feet.

Living in such an unstable world, we tend to have a propensity to worry. Other choices of fear, doubt, and bitterness call us to select their posture when life gets overwhelming. Yet God offers us another choice. Through Him we can dare to hope—not in the government, our family, a job, or even the church. God calls us to surrender our wills to His and rest our hope in Him alone.

Sometimes I get moving through life at a breakneck pace and forget to be daring with hope. I command the calendar, devote time to work, drive the kids around, do some laundry, take care of other chores and errands, make plans for dinner, check in with friends, and then get up tomorrow and start all over again. I need a caution light as I'm racing through life to wake me up and say, "Slow down and pay attention!"

I got one of these wake-up calls recently while driving. Instead of a caution light, I got a caution bump. I had just dropped my girls off at a school activity and was on my way home. Earlier I had dumped out my purse on the passenger seat, frantically looking for something I needed at a moment's notice. Now I was stopped at a red light, and I leaned over to put things back in my purse. Suddenly I felt a huge jolt as my van bumped into the minivan in front of me. I slammed the brake down hard, backed up, and went to talk to the woman in front of me. Thankfully, there was no damage to either car, but as I finished the short drive home, I was a little shaken. How could my foot have let up on the brake without me even realizing it? I was so caught up in my task that I slowly let the car slide forward without even being aware of what I was doing.

I laughed with God as I thought about what He has been teaching me through the Book of Jeremiah: I need to pay attention to really important things (like keeping my foot on the brake) instead of letting a small distraction (like my purse contents) put me in danger of hurting myself and others. This is so true in my spiritual life. The minutia of day-to-day life as well as the trials that so frequently present themselves put me in danger of missing the hope in God's plans for me.

Other wake-up calls come in my life as I study and understand God's Word better. Lately, I've found the words of the prophet Jeremiah echoing into my life and culture with great relevance. This prophet also found himself in a nation known for materialism, economic crisis, political globalization, and religious plurality. Sound familiar? Francis Schaeffer said it this way,

> What, then should be our message in such a world—to the world, to the church, and to ourselves?

> We do not have to guess what God would say about this because there was a period of history, biblical history, which greatly parallels our day. That is the day of Jeremiah. The book of Jeremiah and the book of Lamentations show how God looks at a culture which knew Him and deliberately turned away.[1]

As we delve into the Book of Jeremiah together, we'll find God calling out to His people. He continually asks them to place their hope in Him instead of political alliances, material possessions, and people. Jeremiah gets his reputation as the "weeping prophet" honestly as he delivers weighty messages full of bad news and cautions for living. Yet if we are willing to delve beneath the surface of God's warnings to His heart of love behind them, we find the underlying message: that hope-filled living is possible even in an unstable world. How do we do this? Where do we start?

Six hope-inspiring themes lift right off the pages of Jeremiah's manuscript. Rather than go through the book chapter by chapter, we will explore these themes that are consistent in many verses throughout the chapters. Jeremiah writes about:

Raising the White Flag (Surrender)
Recognizing Counterfeits and the Real Deal (Idolatry)
Opening Our Ears (Listening)
Staying Spiritually Sensitive (Heart Issues)
Quitting the Blame Game (Personal Responsibility)
Finding the Source of Our Hope (The Promised Messiah)

These themes or guidelines for living will be the focus of our six weeks together in Jeremiah's book.

Options for Study

Over the years I've found that what I put into a Bible study directly correlates to what I get out of it. When I take time to do the homework daily instead of cramming it all into one sitting, God's truths sink deeper as I have more time to reflect and meditate on what God is teaching me. When I am intentional about getting together with other women to watch videos and have discussion, I find that this helps keep me from falling off the Bible study wagon midway. Also, making a point to memorize verses and dig deeper through commentaries greatly benefits my soul.

At other times, however, I have bitten off more than I can chew. When our faith is new, our children are small, or there are great demands on our time because of difficult circumstances, ailing parents, or other challenges, we need to be realistic about what we will be able to finish. So this study is designed with options that enable you to tailor it for your particular circumstances and needs.

1. Basic Study. The basic study includes five days of homework for each week and a weekly group session in which you watch a video and discuss what you are learning together. Each day's homework can be completed in about 20-30 minutes. **Boldface purple** type indicates write-in-the-book questions and activities.

2. Deeper Study. If you want an even deeper study, there is an optional "Read Through Jeremiah" challenge that will take you through the entire Book of Jeremiah in order, providing both context and continuity for your study of the prophet's writings. Watch for the prompts in the margins. Additional Digging Deeper articles are also available online (see AbingdonWomen.com/Jeremiah) for those who would like deeper historical context that will take you to the next level in understanding the days of Jeremiah and their connections to our modern world. Finally, memory verses are provided for each week of study so that you may meditate on and memorize key truths from God's Word.

3. Lighter Commitment. If you are in a season of life in which you need a lighter commitment, I encourage you to give yourself permission to do what you can do. God will bless your efforts and speak to you through this study at every level of participation.

> Take some time right now to pray and decide which study option is right for you. Then fill in the circles next to the aspects of the study God is calling you to complete. Be realistic, but also allow yourself to be stretched and challenged as the Holy Spirit directs.

O Make the group sessions a priority. Watch the video and engage in discussion and group learning.

O Complete as much of the homework as you can between sessions.

O Complete all five days of homework between sessions.

O Memorize the memory verse(s) (1-2 verses for each week of lessons).

O Take the "Read Through Jeremiah" challenge, which will guide you in reading through the entire book over the course of the study.

O Read the additional Digging Deeper articles found online that give additional insights and information on related topics.

Be sure to let someone in your group know which parts of the study you plan to do so that you have some accountability and encouragement.

A Final Word

Jeremiah's message was not a popular one. Unfortunately, the people of Judah did not see the hope in God's plans for them, and they did not heed Jeremiah's warnings. Their failure to make life changes in light of God's call to hope in Him led to exile. My prayer is that we will not be like them. I pray that God's timeless truths from this ancient book will help us take a careful look at our lives as we slow down and examine where we might be off course and how we can get back on track.

In the ninth chapter of Jeremiah, we find God calling specifically to women with His truth:

> *Listen, you women, to the words of the Lord;*
> *open your ears to what he has to say.*
> *Teach your daughters to wail;*
> *teach one another how to lament.*
>
> Jeremiah 9:20

God is calling us to open our ears to Him as well. He knows life can throw us curveballs, and He knows how easy it is to get swept away with the cultural current of despair. Jeremiah dared to hope—even when his family rejected him. He lost his home and was mocked, imprisoned, and unjustly accused. He lost friends and finances. His circumstances remained bitter, but he learned to keep his heart soft and hopeful in the midst of tough stuff. As we study together, may we be able to say with Jeremiah:

> *Yet I still dare to hope*
> *when I remember this:*
>
> *The faithful love of the Lord never ends!*
> *His mercies never cease.*
> *Great is his faithfulness;*
> *his mercies begin afresh each morning.*
>
> Lamentations 3:21-23

Are you in need of fresh mercies today? Then get ready to embark on a journey to find God's promise of hope for your life and your circumstances. I dare you to hope!

Melissa

> "For I know the plans I have for you," says the LORD. "They are plans for good and not for disaster, to give you a future and a hope."
>
> Jeremiah 29:11

Week 1

RAISING THE WHITE FLAG

Surrender

Memory Verse

"When I discovered your words, I devoured them.
    They are my joy and my heart's delight,
for I bear your name,
    O LORD God of Heaven's Armies."

Jeremiah 15:16

Day 1: No Excuses

As we meet Jeremiah in this study, we'll find out why he is called the most "psychological of the prophets and at the same time the most interesting as a man."[1] He was a lot like you and me. He got depressed, made excuses, and even did some whining occasionally. However, what sets him apart from most of us is his unrelenting commitment to communicate God's message.

Although Jeremiah's words resound from over 2,600 years ago, they echo into our day with uncanny relevance. As I noted in the introduction, Francis Schaeffer agreed. Recognizing in the 1960s that our world was entering a "post-Christian" era, he made an observation that bears repeating:

> What, then should be our message in such a world—to the world, to the church, and to ourselves?

> We do not have to guess what God would say about this because there was a period of history, biblical history, which greatly parallels our day. That is the day of Jeremiah. The book of Jeremiah and the book of Lamentations show how God looks at a culture which knew Him and deliberately turned away.[2]

Since the time that Schaeffer wrote those words, how much further do you think we have come as a nation from living in close fellowship with our Creator? What are some indicators in our society that reveal a divergence from God's ways?

Digging Deeper

When did Jeremiah's ministry take place? Who were his contemporaries? Which kings ruled during his forty years of prophesying? To get a grasp of where his account fits in God's larger story of hope, go to AbingdonWomen.com/Jeremiah and read Digging Deeper Week 1: "Where Does Jeremiah Fit in the Biblical Timeline?"

The changing of a culture starts with the individuals who are living within it. If we long to see a turning back to God in our land, then we need to recognize that it starts with you and me. Not only does Jeremiah's prophecy matter today; God Himself gives us some direct instructions regarding it.

Read 2 Peter 1:19-21 in the margin. What must we do to the writings of the prophets?

Because of that experience, we have even greater confidence in the message proclaimed by the prophets. You must pay close attention to what they wrote, for their words are like a lamp shining in a dark place—until the Day dawns, and Christ the Morning Star shines in your hearts.

Above all, you must realize that no prophecy in Scripture ever came from the prophet's own understanding, or from human initiative. No, those prophets were moved by the Holy Spirit, and they spoke from God

2 Peter 1:19-21

Jesus also "weighed in" on the study of prophecy. Read Matthew 5:17-19. What did Jesus say that He came to do in regard to the messages of Jeremiah?

As we embark on a journey into the longest and what most consider to be one of the most disorganized books (chronologically speaking) in Scripture, we will be tempted to make excuses about our biblical illiteracy. We are not alone. The Book of Jeremiah begins with a glimpse into his own tendency to excuse his ability to obey God's call. Jeremiah was the son of a priest living in the small town of Anathoth in the land of Benjamin, the least significant of the twelve tribes of Israel. He emerged during a time of great political upheaval. Babylon, Egypt, and Assyria rivaled for world domination, and the land of Judah was shuffled back and forth between them as vassals paying tribute to keep from being destroyed. God called Jeremiah to deliver His messages during the thirteenth year of King Josiah's reign in the land of Judah.

As we look at God's calling on Jeremiah's life in Chapter 1, what encouragement did God give him in verses 4-5?

God assured Jeremiah that He knew him even in the womb. Psalm 139 gives a similar picture from David's pen.

Read Psalm 139:13-14 in the margin. What does David say to the Lord?

If Jeremiah and King David were known and called even *in utero*, what does that tell us about how early and intimately God has known you?

Now, Jeremiah did not hear God's precious words and say, "Yes, sign me up." He had some reservations about speaking God's messages to the people of Judah. Remember the small town and the least tribe that he came from? He had even more concerns about his ability to be used by God, set apart from the womb or not.

What excuses did Jeremiah make in verse 6 of Chapter 1?

We, too, make our fair share of excuses when it comes to obeying God. I know I have come up with some good ones: I'm both too old and too young, I don't have time, and I am not qualified. These are just a few of the excuses I made to the Lord when I felt Him calling me to write this study. At other times I've felt nudges to do something big for God and then talked myself out of it. In Christian circles, ambition to do something big can be labeled as pride or self-promotion. Somehow we convince ourselves that humility means staying under the radar and not attempting anything great for God. Like Jeremiah, we want an "out" to disobey.

What are some excuses you've made when God has called you?

You may be thinking, *I'm not sure God has ever called me to do anything;* but God has a calling on each of our lives. Let's look at what He asked of Jeremiah.

What instructions did God give Jeremiah in verses 7-10 and 17 of Chapter 1?

> God's mission for us as followers of Jesus is very similar to Jeremiah's call. God wants us to go when and where He sends, speak His words, and prepare for action without fear.

God asked Jeremiah to speak His messages. God's mission for us as followers of Jesus is very similar to Jeremiah's call. God wants us to go when and where He sends, speak His words, and prepare for action without fear. How many people do you know who live like this? Often we are prone to give up with the least amount of resistance. Insecurity and fear of failure can keep us from trying new things. We wonder if others will think we are prideful. We question if we really heard God correctly. God knows following Him can be scary for us in our humanness. He told Jeremiah twice, in verses 8 and 17, "Do not be afraid." He wants us to face our fears and trust Him.

Dr. Jennifer Degler, co-author of the book *No More Christian Nice Girl*, says, "Many times we find that women get a pass on not being courageous. . . . We want to call that 'having a gentle and kind spirit,' but really it can be timidity or fear that's holding us back."[3] We also fail to encourage others to step out in faith with bold moves. The success of another—or even the potential that another might be greatly used of God—threatens our own worth, so we talk each other down. Instead we should be encouraging each other to listen to God and then step out in obedience.

God knows His callings can be scary. He doesn't give us marching orders and a slap on the back and then fling us out to figure things out on our own.

What did God do and say to encourage Jeremiah in verses 9 and 17-19 of Chapter 1?

Wow! God makes us strong. He will be with us and take care of us. Even when the task seems too big for us, God assures us that He will not leave us without His help.

As we close today, take some time to reflect and ask God what He is calling you to do in this season of your life (family, career,

ministry, evangelism, using your gifts and talents). Make some notes below:

Think also about your big dreams or aspirations that surface in your thoughts from time to time. List some of them below:

Talk with God

God has a purpose for each of our lives. He has big plans for us. Sadly we often miss it because of our own fear, insecurity, and excuses. Craig Groeschel says in *The Christian Atheist* that "before you can tap into God's life-changing power, you have to eliminate the excuses."[4] Take some time before our Lord. Lay your excuses at His feet and ask Him to make the next steps of obedience to His calling in your life clear right now. Make some brief notes in the margin if you like to share with the group about what you hear from God.

Day 2: Surrender and Popularity

When I was in junior high, my mom told me not to worry about popularity because once you leave high school, no one cares about that stuff anymore. She was wrong. I see it in the neighborhood. I see it at PTO meetings. I see it in the church. Women size each other up all the time. A blend of confidence, money, career success (your own or your husband's), appearance, education, and experience (even in ministry) all contribute to your "status" in whatever social circles you run. If anything, it gets more complicated as you grow older. We are still trying to find the right "lunch table" at every stage of life.

As we continue in our study of Jeremiah, we quickly discover that God is not as concerned about our popularity as He is with our faithfulness to His message. In Numbers, the people of Israel were told to go in and take the Promised Land, but they chose to wander instead. In Jeremiah, we see that God gave a very different message: admit defeat without a fight. Jeremiah's words fail to win him popularity. We can understand why.

Imagine the day the twin towers of the World Trade Center fell. Now pretend the people responsible for such brutality launched a full-scale

Read Through Jeremiah:

Read Jeremiah 1.

Fun Fact:

"Jeremiah's name, not uncommon in Israel, is of disputed meaning. It has been rendered 'Yahweh [The LORD] hurls' (cf. Exod. 15:1), 'the LORD founds,' 'the LORD establishes,' or 'the LORD exalts.'" [5]

attack upon our land. Suppose one of the great Christian leaders of our day began preaching that we should admit defeat without a fight.

What would your initial response be to such a person and message?

Now, remember that Jeremiah was the young, unknown son of a priest from a small town and tribe. No wonder he didn't jump up and down at the task set before him. His message foretold the destruction of their communities. Yet Jeremiah faithfully proclaimed God's words over and over, and he began to get a reputation as a prophet of doom and gloom. This didn't go over well with the government officials.

Read Jeremiah 38:2-3 in the margin and fill in the statements below:

Everyone who stayed in the city to defend their land would

_____.

Everyone who surrendered to the enemy would _____.

Babylon was nipping at Judah's heels, demanding tribute, taking their best people (like Daniel), and threatening total destruction. Jeremiah's suggestion to fully give in didn't sit well with a government that was trying to rally its fighting men and boost morale.

"This is what the Lᴏʀᴅ says: 'Everyone who stays in Jerusalem will die from war, famine, or disease, but those who surrender to the Babylonians will live. Their reward will be life. They will live!'

The Lᴏʀᴅ also says: 'The city of Jerusalem will certainly be handed over to the army of the king of Babylon, who will capture it.'"

Jeremiah 38:2-3

In our lives as well, the message of surrender is not as popular as the message of victory. We want God to fix our circumstances and tell us everything is going to work out fine. We want our money problems solved, our physical illnesses healed, our relationships simplified. While sometimes God chooses to intervene in those ways, other times He calls us to surrender. Ultimately He gives us victory through that surrender. He teaches us things, develops our character, and draws us close to Him through our struggles.

These prophecies in Jeremiah give us much more than just a history of how Judah rebelled against God and faced punishment. While their story warns us to live righteous lives in obedience to God, it is so much more. Its great significance is clearly stated in the last pages of the canonical Word.

Read Revelation 19:10 in the margin. What does this verse tell us is the essence of all prophecy?

> Then I fell down at his feet to worship him, but he said, "No, don't worship me. I am a servant of God, just like you and your brothers and sisters who testify about their faith in Jesus. Worship only God. For the essence of prophecy is to give a clear witness for Jesus."
>
> **Revelation 19:10**

We cannot miss this truth: God's intent in prophecy is to give us a clear picture of our Messiah. Jesus is all over the pages of Jeremiah from start to finish. Although it may come in whispers, hints, foreshadowing, and messianic prophecies, we now have the fullness of God's Word and the hindsight to connect the spiritual dots. How I praise God for allowing me to live at a time in history with access to so much of His truth at my fingertips.

The New Testament sheds further light on how the gospel carries a message of surrender.

Read Luke 9:23 in the margin. What does Christ say that we must do? How often must we do it?

This message of surrender is not a "one-time" salvation experience. It is a daily message for believers.

Just last week I was asking God to lead me in whether to help a single mom on welfare by taking her to lunch and giving her a gift card. My close friend who had a connection with her before I did felt that we should demonstrate tough love and not enable her because of some particular choices she had made recently. I struggled. I prayed. I read Scripture to look for guidance. I asked God to confirm His leading. As a consummate people-pleaser, it was hard to surrender to God's call to help the woman even when I knew my friend might not be happy with my decision. She truly wanted to help the woman as well but felt that God was calling her to keep her distance. (My friend ended up being totally fine with my decision; the battle was more in my insecurity than in reality.)

Just as God called John the Baptist to fast and Jesus to feast, He sometimes has us follow different directions for His purposes. We need to stay close to Him so that we can hear. While

> Then he said to the crowd, "If any of you wants to be my follower, you must turn from your selfish ways, take up your cross daily, and follow me."
>
> **Luke 9:23**

God led His people to go in and conquer the land with Joshua, through Jeremiah His message was "surrender."

In what area(s) of your life is God calling you to surrender? Check all that apply:

____ making amends with anyone you are at odds with

____ tithing to your church

____ getting up earlier so you can pray / setting aside another time to pray

____ obeying Christ in an area that you know won't be popular

____ becoming involved in or stepping down from a ministry because God says to

____ other:

Delivering and obeying God's message of surrender takes faith and obedience. And once we've taken that step, it is often tested by fire.

Turn to Jeremiah 38:4-6 to see what happened to Jeremiah as a result of his faithfulness to the message. Where did he end up?

Sometimes even when we obey completely, we end up in a pit.

Sometimes even when we obey completely, we end up in a pit. The pit, or cistern, was literal for Jeremiah. One source explains, "A cistern was a large pit cut into rock and covered with plaster. It was used to gather rainwater in the winter for use during the dry summer (cf. 2:13). This cistern was so deep that they had to lower Jeremiah into it by ropes. Possibly because of the prolonged drought (cf. 14:1-4) the cistern had no water in it. All it contained was the mud that collected in the bottom of the pit from the dirt carried there by the rain."[6] He could starve or freeze waiting for death in this solitary place.

When you have followed God, have your trials ever seemed to increase? Try to think of a specific incident to share with the group, and make notes below:

Read Through Jeremiah:

Read Jeremiah 2.

Even when we commit to God's message, life still happens. Friends betray us. Husbands leave. Jobs are lost. Health declines instead of improves. These are the times when we must trust God's greater plan even though our circumstances are screaming foul. Obedience should be rewarded, right? Jeremiah honestly dialogued with God over questions such as this, as we will see in the next few days. However, he ultimately surrendered to God's way even when it made no human sense. Thankfully, Jeremiah's story doesn't end in the bottom of a cistern.

What does Jeremiah 38:7-13 reveal about God's commitment to take care of Jeremiah (made in Chapter 1)?

When we are in the pit because of our obedience, we must continue to surrender to God. God even says we have cause to be happy about it.

Read Matthew 5:11-12 in the margin. What is our cause to be happy?

"God blesses you when people mock you and persecute you and lie about you and say all sorts of evil things against you because you are my followers.

Be happy about it! Be very glad! For a great reward awaits you in heaven. And remember, the ancient prophets were persecuted in the same way."

Matthew 5:11-12

When you are experiencing difficulty because of your obedience to God, remember Jeremiah's unpopular message and rough times. Then recall God's faithfulness to take care of him.

Jeremiah told the people that God was calling them to surrender completely. God wanted to save and rescue them, but first they had to surrender. Similarly, we need to yield completely to Christ. He wants to give us rich, satisfying, abundant life (John 10:10). And He knows we won't find it apart from Him.

Talk with God

Jeremiah learned that surrendering to God brings peace and purpose even in the midst of terrifying circumstances. Write a personal prayer of surrender in the margin.

Day 3: Confirmation

As I read through Jeremiah's book, I am amazed at how clearly and boldly he proclaimed God's call to surrender. Over and over he said things like, "Then the Lord spoke to me again," "The Lord gave me another message," "Then the Lord said to me," "This is what the Lord says."

Did God speak to Jeremiah with an audible voice? Were the words written out for him like the Ten Commandments carved in stone? Was it just an inner voice saying, "Jeremiah, I have another message for you"?

Jeremiah seemed to hear God's voice so clearly; he consistently spoke a bold message straight from God. He was chosen as God's anointed prophet and spent a lifetime writing the words contained in this book of Scripture. In total the book contains around ninety separate revelations from God over the span of forty years.

When in your life have you thought God was telling you something, but you weren't sure it was His voice?

Fun Fact:

Jeremiah was a contemporary of these prophets:

Zephaniah
Obadiah
Huldah (prophetess)
Daniel (Babylon)
Ezekiel (Babylon)

Jeremiah spoke with assurance because he allowed God to confirm His messages. Let's glimpse into Jeremiah's intimate prayer life and look for specific ways he knew God was speaking to him. We see in Jeremiah 20 that the priest in charge of the Temple, Pashhur, had just learned of Jeremiah's prophecy calling for surrender and defeat. He arrested Jeremiah and had him whipped and put in stocks. Although Jeremiah was released the next day and continued to preach destruction, he had some heavy questions for his Lord.

In Jeremiah 20:7-18, we find a conflicted man. On the next page, list his statements of hope versus despair:.

Hope	Despair

What does Jeremiah's dialogue with his God reveal about their relationship?

Jeremiah talked with God from a very honest place. When he was confused, he asked questions. When he didn't understand, he rehearsed the character of God.

Think about the time you identified when you weren't sure about God's instructions in your life. What do you learn from Jeremiah's example that you could practically implement when God's messages seem unclear or confusing?

Read Jeremiah 20:9 in the margin. Jeremiah reminded himself that he knew these messages did not originate with him. What did he compare them to?

> *But if I say I'll never mention the LORD*
> *or speak in his name,*
> *his word burns in my heart like a fire.*
> *It's like a fire in my bones!*
> *I am worn out trying to hold it in!*
> *I can't do it!*
>
> **Jeremiah 20:9**

When God asks me to do things I don't want to do (confront people, take bold steps that could be misunderstood, write Bible studies on difficult topics, and so on), I usually resist at first. When I finish making excuses and arguing with Him and finally surrender to His voice, I have a peace in my soul that literally feels like a weight has been lifted. I smile when I should frown. He holds me together when I should be falling apart.

Has God ever given you instructions and you could get no peace until you followed through?

If so, think of an example to share with the group. What did God ask you to do? Why did you resist? What did you experience when you obeyed?

When God tells us something specific, it should happen.

God confirms His voice to us as we honestly wrestle with Him and rehearse His character and Word to combat our conflicted emotions. Then we experience God's peace when we follow His leading.

There is one other important element that we need to explore in looking for confirmation. Read the next statement out loud: *When God tells us something specific, it should happen.*

I can think of times in my life that I clearly heard God's voice. All four of my children struggle with asthma. Many nights I have sat up listening to them breathe, trying to discern whether to call 911 or wait it out until morning. One particular night my five-year-old daughter had a horrible night exchanging air in her wheezy lungs and also felt an intense pain in her side. By morning I drove to the emergency room, unsure whether something was seriously wrong or this would be just another day of asthma breathing treatments.

After X-rays, blood tests, and a visit from a surgeon, there still were no clear answers; and my "momma radar" told me my lethargic daughter was very ill. Shortly after a CAT scan revealed double pneumonia and a lung full of fluid, her organs began to shut down as she went into septic shock. We later found out that the fluid had been infected with a strep virus that had become more than her body could fight off. However, while doctors rushed around her room hooking her body up to machines and calling out medications and dosages, I stood in the midst of what seemed like a medical TV show episode and heard God speak these words very clearly to me: "She will not die." I thought He said it audibly because it was so clear, and so I looked around at the many doctors and nurses flooding the room to see if they had heard it, too. It was unmistakable. For those hours when I should have fallen apart, I felt God's peace and lightness.

When our pastor arrived with my husband, Sean, to pray with us, I was embarrassed that I laughed when Sean tried to warn me that she might not make it through the night. I knew what God had said so clearly and believed it with all my heart. Of course, in the weeks to follow, I allowed myself to worry over her health during much smaller setbacks in her recovery. But in that moment I definitely heard God's voice, and He confirmed it with a miraculous healing of my daughter.

Other times God's voice has not been so clear. A dear friend of mine was struggling with infertility. I prayed almost every day for her, and when I read Scripture that spoke of the blessing of children, I would write her name in the margin of my Bible. One day I thought I heard God say in my spirit that she would get pregnant. "Do you mean this month, Lord? What are you saying?" I asked. When she didn't get pregnant that month, I wondered if I had heard incorrectly. I was concerned about telling my friend what I thought I had heard and giving her false hope. Several months later she underwent a medical procedure, and thankfully, she now has a beautiful baby boy. She did become pregnant, but it was on God's timetable.

How can we tell if God is speaking to us in that still, small voice as we seek Him in prayer or if we are hearing things we want to hear to give ourselves permission to do what we want to do? Did God say our church would grow, or do I just want that to be true? Did God bring that friend to mind because I need to call and check on her, or is that just my crazy brain in overdrive? Does God want me to buy these things, or does He have a different plan for this money He has entrusted to me?

What are you seeking guidance from the Lord about right now?

Have you heard Him speak any words of direction?

In Jeremiah 32, God gives us an example of one way we can know we are on the right track.

Read Jeremiah 32:6-15. What confirmation does verse 8 provide?

What was God trying to tell His people who were headed into captivity through this message? (v. 15)

God wanted the people to know that even though He was going to allow them to suffer, there was still hope for future generations. His desire was not for them to be destroyed but for them to turn from their sin. God's message for His people was hope through surrender. One day God would bring the people back, and they would buy and sell houses again. And the proof would be that what God had said would come to pass.

God told Jeremiah his cousin would come, and he did. The Lord offered proof that His Words would come true. He said the confirmation would come through the events He prophesied through Jeremiah actually happening.

How do 2 Chronicles 36:17-21 and Ezra 1:1-4 validate two of Jeremiah's messages or prophecies?

When God says something will happen, it does— 100 percent of the time.

Many voices shout at us that they have the words of God. When people claim they have heard God say something, it should happen. When God says something will happen, it does—100 percent of the time.

My friend didn't get pregnant the month I thought she might. I had not heard God's voice clearly; I had heard what I desperately wanted to be true.

As followers of Christ there are some messages we don't have to question. We don't have to walk into a store and say, "God, should I steal today?" He has given us His Word with directions and examples for how to live. The message of His gospel does not have to be questioned—God's love, humanity's sin, Christ's death on the cross, and our need to receive Christ personally are clear through Scripture (read Romans for a non-Cliff notes version). Our commission to tell others the good news is also clear. Yet we need the Spirit's clear leading on how and when to invest in others to be able to share that message.

As we listen to God's voice about how we should spend our time, what job we should take, whether we should have another baby, what ministry He is calling us to, or what kind of education is right for our children, we need to look for God to confirm His messages in our lives.

Most often in my life God uses His Word to bring confirmation. Whether I receive a confirming word in a sermon, through a friend, or in my personal daily readings, it is always too clear to be a coincidence. Other times God uses circumstances to confirm His Word. When my daughter was healed from septic shock, it revealed the truth of God's promise. Another time my husband and I heard God say He would provide for a need, and we received a gift for the exact amount the next day. Our God loves to show Himself real to us as we listen for His voice. When we seek Him for confirmation, we will find Him faithful.

Talk with God

Ask God to give you clear leading in whatever area of your life you are seeking answers. Bring Him all your questions and complaints, and then rehearse back to yourself what you know to be true about Him. Be sure to ask Him to give you the mercy of confirmation so that you may know you are on the right track of obedience. *"peace"*

Read Through Jeremiah:

Read Jeremiah 3.

Day 4: Defining Success

In Western Christianity, "success" in ministry is often measured by how many people attend your church or event, how many dedicated themselves to Christ, and how cool and trendy you go about it. We want to see results from the work we do for God. If we don't, then we think we must be doing something wrong.

Of course, we want our lives to have meaning and purpose. God created us with vision, drive, a work ethic, and dreams. These things are not inherently bad. However, we need to evaluate our measuring rod for what constitutes success.

Whether we're aware of it or not, this is where a version of the prosperity gospel sometimes subtly infiltrates the church. I find this thinking creeping into my own soul at times: I follow God = everything should go well for me. But this is not biblical. The list is long of those who followed God and found hardship and difficulty. Job is a classic example. David lived in caves. Joseph was thrown in a pit and wrongly accused. Jesus ended His ministry with exponentially fewer followers than He had at one time and a gruesome death on a cross. Jeremiah also followed God and encountered difficulty.

Throughout Jeremiah's writings, we see his emotions and an example of what he was thinking as he struggled to pursue God radically.

Read the following passages and indicate whether each statement about Jeremiah's emotional state and circumstances is true (T) or false (F):

Jeremiah 8:18–9:2

____ His heart was broken.

____ He was overcome with grief because of the hurt of his people.

____ He questioned God's lack of healing.

____ He expressed excitement about learning from his trials.

____ He wished he could run away and live in a traveler's shack in the desert.

Jeremiah 11:18–12:3

____ God told him people from his own hometown were plotting his murder.

____ He asked God for vengeance against these people.

____ Jeremiah brought complaints to God about why the wicked prosper.

____ Jeremiah was trusting of all people and didn't judge them.

____ He rehearsed the truth that God knows everyone's heart including his own.

Jeremiah related his responses to real-life fears and threats with gut-wrenching honesty. He didn't stuff his feelings about what he was going through.

Are you currently struggling with frustration or depression in your life? If so, what are some underlying causes you can identify?

Write a few sentences below, pouring out any frustrations you have over the results of your attempts to follow God in your current circumstances.

As you evaluate your life, remember that some circumstances are just difficult. God didn't expect Jeremiah to celebrate the sin of his people, death threats, or rumors spread about him. He doesn't want you to pretend your own problems are of no consequence. He created you with emotions that respond to circumstances.

In a recent trial over a broken friendship, I lost my appetite and struggled to sleep. I cried all the time. I questioned whether I was trusting God because my physical and emotional reactions were so strong.

Jeremiah, however, shows us that even the most faithful followers can feel anxiety and depression and struggle to believe God through rough circumstances. God invites us to come to Him and wrestle through our personal battles. These struggles don't mean we are unsuccessful Christians. Instead, they give us an opportunity to take our thoughts and emotions to God. We must resist the urge to numb ourselves with food, television, and any other distraction that keeps us from dealing with our pain. As we live in a world marred by sin, we need prayer, God's Word, and sometimes a good counselor to help us sort out the very real trials that ravage our lives.

As you think about Jeremiah's responses to the difficulties he encountered, what steps do you need to take in order to deal with the pain in your own life in a healthier, biblical way?

> *Even the most faithful followers can feel anxiety and depression and struggle to believe God through rough circumstances. God invites us to come to Him and wrestle through our personal battles. These struggles don't mean we are unsuccessful Christians. Instead, they give us an opportunity to take our thoughts and emotions to God.*

Our trials are often seasonal and temporary. However, Jeremiah's ministry did not have a happily-ever-after ending like the stories of many other great Bible heroes. David lived in caves but eventually was crowned king. Joseph labored in prison but was elevated to second in command over all Egypt. Jeremiah is called the weeping prophet because the message God gave him was difficult. It wasn't fun to deliver. People didn't listen.

Jeremiah was imprisoned, mocked, put in a cistern, and eventually taken to Egypt against his will. He didn't end up on top with a great life after a few years of difficulty. Though he seemed unsuccessful according to the world's standards, he was very accomplished in God's economy. He lived for God's kingdom, followed God's instructions, and stayed true to the words God gave Him to speak. He was successful in God's eyes because he was faithful and obedient. In eternity Jeremiah can look back on his rough road in life knowing that He lived it well even though it wasn't easy.

> *"Yes," Jesus replied, "and I assure you that everyone who has given up house or brothers or sisters or mother or father or children or property, for my sake and for the Good News,*
>
> *will receive now in return a hundred times as many houses, brothers, sisters, mothers, children, and property—along with persecution. And in the world to come that person will have eternal life.*
>
> *But many who are the greatest now will be least important then, and those who seem least important now will be the greatest then."*
>
> Mark 10:29-31

Read Mark 10:29-31 in the margin. How do Jesus' words encourage us to allow Him to stamp eternity in our eyes instead of living for the fleeting pleasures of today?

What does He say about the greatest and the least?

How have you been defining success in your life recently?

Fill in the blank:

If I could just _____,

then I would be happy with my life.

In the Western church and culture, we tend to want instant gratification and to measure success by immediate results. Did it "work"? What did/do people think? Do my kids behave, get good grades, and excel in sports? Are others impressed with my nice home? Do I have enough status in my job? When will I get a promotion? These are the outward measures of doing it right in our culture.

God's standards of success, on the other hand, are not the same as ours. We might follow God wholeheartedly and still lose our job, get sick, or face financial ruin. We may not look to others like the greatest now, but God says that those who sacrifice their wills for His will be great in heaven.

Do you tend to see trials and problems as punishment and good circumstances as reward? Why or why not?

If so, ask God to reveal where your way of thinking might be out of line with His. Write your thoughts below.

Read Matthew 5:1-12. How does God describe the blessed life or individual, and how does this differ from our culture's definition of success?

Our culture says "blessed are those who are rich, happy, proud, selfish, self-indulgent, critical, promiscuous, demanding, and rewarded." Jesus says "blessed are the pure" (v. 8 NIV). Our world says to mix in a little "bad girl." God's standards starkly contrast what our media and culture label as desirable. He blesses those who are poor, sorrowful, humble, hungry for what is right, merciful, pure, peaceable, and persecuted.

What does Matthew 5:12 say about those who are like the persecuted prophets?

Fun Fact:

The Book of Jeremiah is not arranged chronologically.

God's standards starkly contrast what our media and culture label as desirable.

Read Through Jeremiah:

Read Jeremiah 4.

What does this tell us about Jeremiah?

What can help us walk in faith and obedience despite trials and a lack of worldly success, waiting for eternal rewards and results?

Today has been a heavy day as we have looked at the world's definition of success versus God's definition of success. Tomorrow we will end this week on a hopeful note, focusing on the truth that even though God allows us to experience trials, He promises to be with us and take care of us through them. Though Jeremiah's life was difficult, may we not forget that it was truly blessed.

Talk with God

Think now about some recent experiences that haven't seemed "successful" by our culture's standards. Talk with God about how these difficulties have impacted your relationship with Him and others. Give thanks for at least one or more good things that have come out of those circumstances. Make notes in the margin.

Day 5: White Flag Anxiety

I felt sick to my stomach with fear and anxiety. I had just found out that the school district where our church and four other church plants hold services is doubling the rental rates. This came at the same time when support from our sending church ended and offerings were down. I was freaking out. *Where does a church planter's wife go to resign?* I wondered. *Can you quit a job that has no monetary compensation?*

Then, as I lay on my face asking God what He was doing, He told me to think about what I was going to be writing for this week of study. He never promises easy circumstances, as we witnessed yesterday. Jeremiah faced one difficult situation after another. He struggled with depression. He was left in a cistern to die. He knew that according to God's messages, the people of Israel were facing seventy years of captivity. Yet in the midst of it all, he clung to the Lord. He trusted in God to take care of him.

Read Jeremiah 15:10-18 and write some of Jeremiah's complaints below. (See vv. 10, 15, and 18.)

Jeremiah didn't try to sugarcoat his pain. He boldly told God that he wished he were never born. He called God's help uncertain and blamed Him for the suffering he endured. He held nothing back.

What are your current complaints before your God? Keep it real. God already knows what you really feel; He invites you to tell Him and ask hard questions.

After Jeremiah brought his complaints, he waited for God to respond. Read Jeremiah 15:11-14 again, and look also at verses 19-21. What do verses 11 and 21 say that God would do for Jeremiah?

How do these promises from God bring you comfort and faith regarding your own current complaints?

Even though our circumstances may range anywhere from puzzling to downright depressing, we can know that God is the One who will take care of us. He doesn't leave us as orphans in a sea of questions, trials, and difficulties. He promises to walk with us.

Read Jeremiah 15:16-17. As God answered Jeremiah's complaints, what are the two active steps Jeremiah took?

1.

2.

The first thing Jeremiah did was devour God's Word. Though he didn't have access to the entire biblical canon that we are privileged to possess in great abundance, we know he came in contact with the Pentateuch, the first five books of the Bible. These scrolls were rediscovered by King Josiah early in Jeremiah's ministry. The prophets Isaiah and Hosea wrote one hundred years before Jeremiah began to dictate his messages from God to the scribe named Baruch. Glimpses of their influence on Jeremiah evidence themselves in his messages. Word pictures from the psalmists also echo into the pages of his prophecy. Jeremiah devoured God's inspired words like food.

Take a minute to bring this a little closer to home. Jeremiah didn't consume God's Word accidentally. It was an intentional act of his will, not his emotions. (We've seen firsthand that his emotions were much like ours—flittering from despair to hope from one moment to another.) Jeremiah set his will to study God's Word, and his emotions followed truth as he argued and experienced the living Word.

Check at least one action step in the list below that you can act on this week:

____ **Begin attending a church regularly that faithfully preaches God's Word.**

____ **Set a goal of where and when you will meet with God in His Word each day and for how long—put it on the calendar you live from whether it's your phone, BlackBerry, planner, or home calendar.**

____ **Ask someone to keep you accountable and check in with you weekly about how your time in God's Word is going.**

____ **Find a partner and begin memorizing God's Word.**

____ **Begin a family practice of reading God's Word together— mornings, mealtimes, or bedtimes are great times to read and discuss a short passage, psalm, or proverb.**

____ **This is another way God is calling me to intentionally "devour" His Word:_____**

The second practical step Jeremiah took was to stand alone. Verse 17 says he chose the unpopular route of nonconformity. At the end of verse 19, God clearly called Jeremiah with a powerful passage. I want to write the New Living Translation of this verse on my children's school backpacks!

In each of these translations of Jeremiah 15:19, underline the word that is repeated:

"It is they who must return to you;

   you must not return to them." (HCSB)

"Let this people turn to you,

   but you must not turn to them." (NIV)

"You must influence them;

   do not let them influence you!" (NLT)

> If we want our children or loved ones to be influencers, we must give them an example to follow in our lives.

Though translators used words like *return, turn,* and *influence,* the Hebrew word is *shuwb.* It means "to turn back, to lead away."[7] We should be women who draw others to our God rather than women who are pulled away from Him by our culture. God called Jeremiah to be the influencer. I pray this for my four children who attend public schools where there are all kinds of stimuli.

In order to be the influencer instead of the influenced, Jeremiah devoured God's Word and chose to stand alone. If we want our children or loved ones to be influencers, we must give them an example to follow in our lives. Unfortunately, the tendency to fall in with the crowd didn't end in middle school for any of us. Have you joined in with the crowd regarding media choices, gossip, spending habits, or some other area of life where taking a stand could be unpopular? Where are you being dragged down instead of being a spokeswoman with God's message?

Ask God to bring to mind an area where He needs to shine His light of nonconformity into your life. Name it here:

We have one more passage to consider before we close this week about surrendering to God's message. Don't worry—we're going to end this week on a hopeful note! Let's look at this incredible picture of blessing for those who place their hope in God. He is so worth it. Every trial, frustration, and battle with flesh and sin that leaves us ready to call it quits fades in comparison with the blessing that comes from fully yielding to our Creator God. He paints a picture so that His people won't miss the joy of a life fully yielded to His message. God so desperately doesn't want us to miss this truth about His care for us in the midst of life's trials that He gives us two visuals. We're going to create some labels for these visuals to help these truths stick with us and sink deep into our souls.

The first picture, found in Jeremiah 17:5-8, is the dry shrub for those who trust in human strength. The Hebrew word for trust in this passage is *batach*, which means "a place of refuge" or "safe place."[8] When we make people or anything wrought of human effort our safe place, God lets us know what we have to look forward to. The people in Jeremiah's day chose to trust in political alliances and idolatry. They lost faith in the God of their ancestors. They even looked to Egypt for help—the same country who held them captive as slaves for over four hundred years in the days of Moses. God called them to trust Him and let them know clearly what the results of human help would be.

Read Jeremiah 17:5-8 (in the New Living Translation, if possible). See if you can identify four results described in verse 6 and write them below. Look for the key words shown and choose a word to describe each condition.

1. _____
(key word: stunted)

2. _____
(key words: no hope)

3. _____
(key words: live in barren wilderness, uninhabited)

4. _____
(key words: live in salty land)

God doesn't leave us to wonder what will happen if we make our safe place the government, our jobs, our friendships, or even our families. People die, children grow up, and regimes change. He tells us that we will find ourselves in the condition of being 1) unproductive, 2) hopeless, 3) isolated, and 4) bitter if we place our ultimate trust in anything but Him alone (the words you chose may differ slightly). He says that we will live in a barren wilderness, an uninhabited salty land. But He graciously will do whatever it takes to "wake us up" from this state. God allowed the people of Judah to face destruction and captivity in order to help them see their "barrenness" and how far they had drifted from Him.

Next, God gives us a picture of the other alternative.

Now look at verse 8 and list below the benefits of those who make the Lord their hope and confidence. Again, look for the key words below and choose a word to describe each benefit.

1. _____
(key words: deep roots)

2. _____
(key words: not bothered
by heat/drought)

3. _____
(key words: leaves stay green)

4. _____
(key words: never stop producing fruit)

God tells us that we will be 1) stable, 2) nourished, 3) vibrant/growing, and 4) productive (the words you chose may differ slightly). First we read that deep roots will make us stable. This blessed life will not be problem-free. He honestly tells us we may still encounter heat and long months of drought. However, we won't dry up because His water from the river will nourish us. He promises to keep our leaves green and still produce fruit in our lives.

Read Ezekiel 47:12 in the margin. In Ezekiel's vision of heaven, what additional insight do we get into the purpose of the fruit and the leaves?

> *Fruit trees of all kinds will grow along both sides of the river. The leaves of these trees will never turn brown and fall, and there will always be fruit on their branches. There will be a new crop every month, for they are watered by the river flowing from the Temple. The fruit will be for food and the leaves for healing.*
>
> **Ezekiel 47:12**

What a contrast to the salty shrub is the sweet fruit of the Spirit in our lives, nourishing those around us. Not only will the one who makes the Lord her hope and confidence produce fruit, she also will get to be part of God's plan for healing in this broken world. When we make God our safe place, He will take care of us and use us for His Kingdom work.

As we've seen, Jeremiah's life was not one of comfort, status, and material wealth; but he had great treasure—not only in the next life, but also in his life on earth through blessings, even despite trials.

The blessed life is far better than the circumstantially happy life because it is not dependent on anything but the Lord. Only He is unchanging. Only He is secure. Only He can be fully trusted. The most secure of careers can end tomorrow. The most stable family can be quickly interrupted by divorce or tragedy. When we trust in human resources, we are like a shrub in the desert that dries up and dies. However, when we make the Lord our confidence, we can weather the times of drought and heat.

We need one more artistic moment before we end today. Whether you choose to draw a simple sketch or a gallery-worthy portrait, draw a tree representing your life in the space provided at the top of the next page. Is it close to the river, in the desert, or somewhere in between?

Read Through Jeremiah:

Read Jeremiah 5–6.

We are God's messengers, and He promises to take care of us. He gives us His Word to build our faith and encourage us to trust Him even when it seems like He doesn't care. As a loving Father, He longs to be close to His children. He never forces us to come near, but He calls to us through His Word to put our hope and confidence in Him alone.

Next week we'll take a deeper look into the things that lured the Israelites away from this deep connection with God and see what hope-filled words God might want to speak over us.

Talk with God

Take a few moments with God now and ask Him to show you anything that might be hindering deep connection with Him. Below or beside your tree drawing, write the answer to this question: *What needs to change in your life to move your tree closer to the riverbank?*

Take time to ask God how He wants you to answer this question. Don't skip over it. Remember how Jeremiah brought his complaints and then waited for God to respond? Ask God your hard questions, listen for His voice when He answers you, and then respond to that voice with obedience.

Digging Deeper

What did it mean to be a prophet of God? To learn some of the distinctive marks of a prophet and see a comparison chart, go to AbingdonWomen.com/Jeremiah and read Digging Deeper Week 1: "The Profile of a Prophet."

Video Viewer Guide

WEEK 1: RAISING THE WHITE FLAG

Surrender

We can dare to _hope_ because our God is _faithful_.

Jeremiah 17:5-8 – Stunted shrub in the desert vs. tree planted along the riverbank

Trust – Hebrew *batach*

It means _a safe place_____.

When God is not our safe place, we are like the shrub in the desert.

When we choose to turn to _human strength_____
instead of God . . . we will be _unproductive_.

When we make human strength our "thing" [safe place],

we'll get _hopeless_____.

When we get hopeless and down and negative,

we become _isolated_____.

It was a salty land. A little bit of salt tastes good;

a lot of salt [is] _bitter_____.

VIDEO VIEWER GUIDE: WEEK 1

When we're planted by the riverbank, God is our hope and our confidence.

God says if we'll plant ourselves next to Him,

He's going to make us __stable__ .

__Blind__ is the woman or man who makes the Lord

their hope and their confidence.

God says that we can be __sweet__ when He is the water

flowing up through us.

"Fruit trees of all kinds will grow along both sides of the river. The leaves of these trees will never turn brown and fall, and there will always be fruit on their branches. There will be a new crop every month, for they are watered by the river flowing from the Temple. The fruit will be for food and the leaves for __healing__ *."*

Ezekiel 47:12 NLT

Week 2

RECOGNIZING COUNTERFEITS AND THE REAL DEAL

Idolatry

Memory Verse

Idols are worthless; they are ridiculous lies!
   On the day of reckoning they will all be destroyed.
But the God of Israel is no idol!
   He is the Creator of everything that exists,
including Israel, his own special possession.
   The LORD of Heaven's Armies is his name!
                                      Jeremiah 10:15-16

Day 1: Forgetfulness

The feeling of having forgotten something important is no fun. For ten years, I have unlocked the door and checked people in for a 6:00 a.m. exercise class two days a week. This means I have to get up at 5:30 a.m. to get there in time. (Yes, I often sleep in my workout clothes and roll out of bed, brush my teeth, grab a water bottle, and jump in my car.) I love the other crazy girls that get up early to get a workout finished before it's light outside. A few times I have gotten my days mixed up or not set my alarm correctly. When I wake up and realize that I've overslept and missed my commitment, it starts my whole day off on the wrong note. I've let others down. I forgot something I'm supposed to remember. A friend of mine placed a sticky note right on her steering wheel to help her remember her carpool schedule. Too many times she had forgotten, and she hated the feeling of not getting it right.

Over twenty-five times the words *remind, remember, forget,* or *forgotten* are used in the Book of Jeremiah. God knows our tendency to forget and calls us to intentionally set patterns in our lives to help us remember Him against the backdrop of counterfeit gods screaming for our attention.

While I needed to remember to get my sleepy self out of bed in time for my exercise class and my friend needed to know when to pick up extra children in the carpool, the people of Judah forgot something of much greater magnitude. Their forgetfulness carried intense consequences.

Fun Fact:

King Jehoiakim reigned eleven years in Judah and sponsored idolatry. He strongly opposed Jeremiah's message and ministry.

God knows our tendency to forget and calls us to intentionally set patterns in our lives to help us remember Him....

God's powerful hand that brought the Israelites out of slavery in Egypt also wrote His sacred instructions on tablets of stone. The second commandment on that list of the big ten contains the most detailed explanation of them all.

Read Exodus 20:4-6 in the margin. What are God's directives concerning idolatry?

Now look what God says just a few chapters later in Exodus 23:33 (also in the margin). How does God describe the result of idolatry in our lives?

Some versions of Scripture call idolatry a trap, and others say it's a snare. The Hebrew word for idolatry, *mowqesh*, means bait, trap, snare, or lure.[1] God warns His people that the things of this world will try to lure them away. Like the Sirens in Greek mythology who sang beautiful songs to lure men to their death, so this world sings lies to us that our God is not enough. The bait looks dangerously similar to the real thing so that we will fall for the counterfeit.

Jeremiah called the people to remember their God because the people were listening to the "music" and taking the bait. They couldn't see the rot in their souls. Early in Jeremiah's ministry a short-lived revival had occurred when King Josiah had discovered scrolls containing God's laws during Temple repairs. Though scholars disagree as to exactly which Bible books the scrolls contained, we learn from 2 Kings 22 that during King Josiah's reign reforms were enacted based on a reading of God's words about His strict forbiddance of idolatry. (Many scholars make a case for Deuteronomy as the probable book that was contained in the scrolls, though it could have been portions of Leviticus or Exodus as all three books contain God's laws concerning idolatry.) Shortly after this renewal of faith and turning away from idolatry, however, the people quickly fell back into their old patterns of sin.

God gives two examples to contrast the forgetfulness of His people in Jeremiah 2:32. Read the verse in the margin, and describe the two women and the items they never forget:

I remember staring at my ring during college classes after I got engaged. I could barely concentrate on what my professors were saying about history of doctrine, Western civilization, or even systematic theology with that brilliant thing glowing up at me. I had never worn a ring or much jewelry at all before my future husband offered me a beautiful diamond when he asked me to marry him. Dreaming of a life with him and the hope of what the future held for us sparkled in that band around my finger. You can bet I never forgot about my jewelry then. And how many brides can't remember where they have put their wedding gowns? We take great care with these items because they are important to us.

> *"Does a young woman forget her jewelry?*
> *Does a bride hide her wedding dress?*
> *Yet for years on end my people have forgotten me."*
>
> **Jeremiah 2:32**

What example could God use from your life? Fill in the blanks:

Does _____(your name) ever forget

her _____?

How does God end verse 32?

"Yet for years on end
    my people have _____ _____."

I don't know how you filled in the blank after your name, but sometimes we are more careful with our makeup, cell phones, and workout regimens than with our relationship with the living God. We take greater care to color our gray hairs, accessorize our outfits, and make sure our tans are even than to keep our hearts right with our Creator.

Turn to Jeremiah 11:1-13 and carefully read Jeremiah's message, looking for a word that is continually repeated throughout these verses. Write it below:

God calls them to remember His *covenant*. This word has escaped our vernacular. Covenants in our culture remind us of marriage ceremonies in which a man and woman make a covenant to love each other forever. In a world where more than 50 percent of these vows will not stand the test of time, it is difficult to wrap our minds around what God is saying. He is not like us. He is a promise-keeper. When He says to worship Him alone, He means it. When He says there will be consequences if we don't, He isn't taking it lightly. He wanted the people to remember the covenant they made with Him. He called their idolatry "altars of shame" in verse 13 (NLT).

He is the One who created us, the One who sees the master plan, the God who desires a close relationship with us. The things of this earth that urgently cry out for our attention often relegate God to the bottom of the list. If we call ourselves Christ-followers, then we should agree that our relationship with God should be the number one thing in our lives. Yet many times we forget what is most important because of the lure of things of this world.

> *If we call ourselves Christ-followers, then we should agree that our relationship with God should be the number one thing in our lives. Yet many times we forget what is most important because of the lure of things of this world.*

This is not a new problem. Even without television, magazines, the Internet, and other modern media, the people of Israel were so focused on the things of this earth that they forgot their God. Jeremiah was God's prophet calling out to the people: "Don't forget God because you are so focused on things you can touch, taste, and feel."

Over forty verses scattered throughout the Book of Jeremiah mention idols. Let's look at just a few of them.

Draw a line to match the passage with the corresponding methodology of worship:

13:27	burning incense and pouring out drink offerings
19:4-5	setting up idols in God's Temple
19:13	worshiping idols in the fields and on the hills
32:34	burning incense and children

We can read through the Book of Jeremiah and self-righteously accuse the Israelites. In the verses above they were making things with their own hands and worshiping them instead of God. They participated in adultery, lust, and child sacrifice and spent their time and money pouring out offerings to imaginary gods. Our idolatry may look different today, but the same root lies beneath the surface of our actions.

Read Through Jeremiah:

Read Jeremiah 7.

What are some practices, relationships, or objects in our culture that can become idolatrous when they draw our hearts away from God?

Perhaps these are your personal idols. While they may not be physical statues and your worship may not include pouring out drinks or burning incense, God calls you to keep Him foremost in your life. Though our outward expressions may look different than those in Jeremiah's day, is it possible we have succumbed to our culture's more subtle relationship with idolatry?

An idol is an image we worship. In our culture, however, the word *idol* has taken on a harmless connotation, such as with the television show *American Idol*. In the context of the show, an idol is something to be adored or appreciated. Now, most of us are not worshiping the contestants on *American Idol* but merely enjoying their God-given talent. However, we can set up idols just as easily as the Israelites in Jeremiah's day when we spend more time and effort focusing on anything other than God. Just as God asked the people of Judah to remember Him, He asks the same thing of us. He made a new covenant with us through the blood of His Son, Jesus, and He wants us to remember what He has done.

What are some tools you use to help you remember important things in your life?

How could you utilize the same tools you use to remember meetings, soccer practice, hair appointments, or dates with your significant other to help you keep God at the center of your life?

Fun Fact:

Fun Fact: Jeremiah is thought to have been heavily influenced by the prophet Hosea. The imagery in Chapter 2 of Jeremiah's book is reminiscent of Hosea.

So many other things are calling out for your time and attention. Don't let the minutia of life crowd out the most important thing: your relationship with your Creator. Put a sticky note on your steering wheel with a Scripture verse or a reminder to pray, set an alarm to signal your devotional time, or let your small group or church attendance take priority over your sports commitments. Do whatever it takes to remember the covenant you made the day you asked Christ to take first place in your life. If we aren't intentional, counterfeits will replace God's best for us, and as we'll see tomorrow, they never really satisfy.

Talk with God

Take a moment right now to be still in God's presence. Put aside all thoughts of things you need to do, and quiet your soul. Then ask God to reveal one practical step you can take to remember Him in your day tomorrow. When you hear from God, write your action step for tomorrow in the margin.

Day 2: Spotting a Fake

I remember being at church camp as a teenager and hearing the speaker tell a story of a little girl with a fake pearl necklace. Here is my version of this popular and often-told story.

A little girl bought a plastic pearl necklace with the money she had been saving all year. She loved her pearls and felt so grown up when she wore them. She only took them off when she went swimming or took a bath. Though the pearls weren't real, that didn't matter to her. She had bought them all by herself.

This little girl had a loving father. One day he said to her, "Honey, do you love me?"

"Yes, Daddy," she said. "You know I love you."

"Then will you give me your pearls?" her father asked.

"Not my pearls!" the little girl practically gasped. "But you can have my toy horse."

"That's okay, Sweetheart. I love you," he replied. And then he kissed her cheek.

About a week later, the father asked his little girl again, "Do you love me?"

"Daddy, you know I love you," she said.

"Then will you give me your pearls?" he repeated.

"Not my pearls. But I'll give you my baby doll."

"That's okay. I love you," the father answered. And once again he gave her a kiss on the cheek.

This same routine happened again and again, and the little girl began to wonder, "If Daddy loves me, why does he want to take away something I love?"

Then one day the little girl walked up to her father with tears in her eyes and held out her fake pearl necklace. "Here, Daddy. This is for you," she said.

The father reached out a hand to take the necklace, and with his other hand he reached into his pocket and pulled out a velvet case. Inside that case was a strand of genuine pearls, chosen with love and care for his daughter. He had had the pearls all along but was waiting for his daughter to give up what she had so that he could give her something even better.

As we read God's strong reaction to idolatry in Jeremiah, let's not forget His heart behind it. He sees us settling for a fake when He wants to give us the real thing—and we're not talking about a necklace. The stakes are much higher. They echo into eternity.

The second chapter of Jeremiah lays out clearly God's heart regarding idolatry.

Read Jeremiah 2:1-9. What question did the people and their leaders fail to ask? (vv. 6, 8)

When we neglect to remember all the ways God has shown Himself in our lives, we make ourselves easy prey for the world's counterfeit offerings.

As we saw yesterday, idolatry's precursor is forgetfulness. When we neglect to remember all the ways God has shown Himself in our lives, we make ourselves easy prey for the world's counterfeit offerings. In these verses God warns His people to ask, "Where is the LORD?" We too can become apathetic when our circumstances overwhelm us. Often we turn to people, money, and human wisdom to try to make sense of our problems.

Take a moment to consider something weighing on your heart right now. God wants us to ask the question: *Where is God at work in my situation?* Try to identify at least one way God is revealing Himself to you through this situation or circumstance, and write it here:

*"Go west and look in the land
of Cyprus; go east and search
through the land of Kedar.
Has anyone ever heard of
anything as strange as this?*

*Has any nation ever traded
its gods for new ones,
even though they are not gods at all?
Yet my people have exchanged their
glorious God for worthless idols!*

*The heavens are shocked
at such a thing
and shrink back in horror and dismay,"*
says the Lord.

*"For my people have done
two evil things:
They have abandoned me—
the fountain of living water.
And they have dug for themselves
cracked cisterns
that can hold no water at all!"*

Jeremiah 2:10-13

Now let's look at the next section of Jeremiah 2 and consider what happens when we cling to the world's counterfeits.

Read Jeremiah 2:10-13 in the margin. What is the illustration and message found in these verses?

The fountain of living water and the cracked cisterns are one of the many great physical illustrations God gives to help us understand what happens when we trust in the things we can see and feel instead of yielding ourselves to Him. Like in the story of the fake pearls, we tend to hold tightly to what we think will help us through. We put our trust in people, jobs, status, money, and any number of things that may seem safer to trust than God. We dig in our heels with empty systems that aren't really secure and make our own feeble attempts at feeling safe and loved. It's all just a cracked cistern. Leaky. It's probably filled with sludge and dirty water like the cistern Jeremiah was lowered into that we talked about last week. Yet because it's tangible, we'll settle for it over the fountain of living water.

One commentary points out that "Israel turned to idolatrous objects of trust; Jeremiah compared these with underground water-storage devices for rainwater, which were broken and let water seep out, thus proving useless."[2] Cracked cisterns aren't just damaged. They are completely useless.

In order to identify the cracked cisterns in our lives, we need a modern definition of idolatry. Timothy Keller, author of *Counterfeit Gods*, defines an idol as "anything more important to you than God, anything that absorbs your heart and imagination more than God, anything you seek to give you what only God can give."[3] This idolatry can take two forms:

1. an inherently bad object, practice, or habit
2. a good person, thing, or practice that we elevate above God

Which of these two forms of idolatry do you think is more difficult to identify and why?

Let's start with what I believe is the easier one to recognize—but not necessarily the easier one to overcome!

Read 1 John 5:20-21 in the margin. What are we to keep away from?

What are some things that can take God's place in the hearts of Christ-followers today?

If your idol is an important person or persons in your life such as a husband or children, you obviously can't "stay away" from them. (We will address that kind of idol in just a moment.) However, there are some things we just need to make a clean break from.

Is there a practice, habit, harmful relationship (outside family), media choice, or secret sin that God is calling you to turn your back on in order to keep Him first in your heart? Whether it is a lifetime stronghold or a small, distracting practice, take a moment *right now* to write it on a piece of paper, surrender it to God, and then burn it with a lighter or match. Write a brief note in the margin about the experience.

This exercise may sound silly, but it has been very effective for me. I remember throwing a stick representing a bad habit or sin into a fire at church camp and writing sins on pieces of paper and throwing them in a fire at youth group. I have forgotten the specifics of most of the Bible lessons taught me during my childhood and teenage years, but these times of watching a stick or paper burn have stuck in my mind. They were marked moments when I asked God to light a fire in me. Though there were later struggles and relapses in the areas I had identified, those moments began a journey toward freedom for me.

Ask God to help you remember the flame of your own paper burning and get started on the road to freedom in this area that you identified. Make it a day you will never forget, the day you started a real fire in your living room, kitchen, or wherever you are—both literally and spiritually!

> *God gave us our families, jobs, and ministries as gifts. However, the danger comes when these things become ultimate or deified. If we lose them, ...will we despair?*

Now, let's look at the second form idolatry often takes. Idols can be good things, such as our children, our husbands or significant others, or intangible things such as our appearance, comfort, security, or ability to bring order to our lives (control). Idols also can be time-suckers in our lives, such as TV, social media, or romance novels. There is no end to the list of things that can take God's place in our hearts.

Something crosses the line into idolatry based on its elevation in our heart and mind. God gave us our families, jobs, and ministries as gifts. However, the danger comes when these things become ultimate or deified. If we lose them, we will feel sorrow; but will we despair? If the loss of our status, money, or family member will reduce us to despair, then that person or thing may have begun to take the place of God in our hearts and become an idol.

In *Counterfeit Gods*, Timothy Keller helps us see just how we elevate things above God:

We know a good thing has become a counterfeit god when its demands on you exceed proper boundaries. Making an idol out of work may mean that you work until you ruin your health, or you break the laws in order to get ahead. Making an idol out of love may mean allowing the lover to exploit and abuse you, or it may cause terrible blindness to the pathologies in the relationship. An idolatrous attachment can lead you to break any promise, rationalize any indiscretion, or betray any other allegiance, in order to hold on to it. It may drive you to violate all good and proper boundaries. To practice idolatry is to be a slave.[4]

We are sometimes very skilled at identifying the idols in the lives of those around us, but what can help us recognize when too much of a good thing has become an idol in our own lives?

Think through the following categories and write down anything or anyone that comes to mind that you may be trusting instead of God. Think of where you spend your mental energy, money, and time. Remember that idols may not be inherently bad people or things; they can be good relationships and things that become idolatrous when we allow them to take God's place in our hearts.

People:

Leisure activities/hobbies:

Health:

Ideas:

Jobs/Income:

Material possessions:

Habits:

In Chapter 2 of Jeremiah, we see that God is frustrated that the people would not admit their sin. He already saw it and knew about it. Anything you have written above is no surprise to Him. Confess these idols and ask Him to help you walk in repentance. Like the fake pearls the little girl clenched in her hand, we need to release and surrender what we hold too tightly so that God can give us the real thing: Himself.

On the pages of Scripture it seems so clear, but in the real world it's not so easy. How will we pay the bills? Who will be a loyal friend? Who will help me with a difficult boss? Will I really survive motherhood? Can we trust God to be the fountain, or should we dig a cistern on the side just to be sure?

We need to release and surrender what we hold too tightly so that God can give us the real thing: Himself.

Timothy Keller offers this observation:

Here, then, is the practical answer to our own idolatries, . . . which are not spiritually safe to have and hold. We need to offer them up. We need to find a way to keep from clutching them too tightly, of being enslaved to them. We will never do so by mouthing abstractions about how great God is. We have to know, to be assured, that God so loves, cherishes, and delights in us that we can rest our hearts in him for our significance and security and handle anything that happens in life.[5]

Only in embracing God as the fountain of living water are we able to stop trusting in our cracked cisterns.

In order to identify and smash our idols, we must realize God wants to give us the real thing. The cracked cistern doesn't even begin to compare with the fountain God offers.

Write Jeremiah 2:11b below:

God has not changed His mind on this topic. When we elevate people, stuff, status, or anything our culture promotes for fulfillment, we exchange our glorious God for counterfeits.

Jesus replied, "Anyone who drinks this water will soon become thirsty again.

But those who drink the water I give will never be thirsty again. It becomes a fresh, bubbling spring within them, giving them eternal life."

John 4:13-14

Read John 4:13-14 in the margin. What does Jesus say about the water He offers?

How does the water Jesus offers differ from the water that might be collected in a cracked cistern?

God uses the illustration of the fountain and the cracked cistern in Chapter 2, but by Chapter 51 He uses the strongest possible language.

Read Jeremiah 51:17-19 in the margin. (This passage may seem familiar; it repeats words found in Jeremiah 10:15-16, our memory verse.) What does this passage tell us about the God we worship?

Read Through Jeremiah:

Read Jeremiah 8–9.

In order to stop our apathetic satisfaction with substitutes, we need to find satisfaction in the true Creator God. He truly is satisfying. He offers the real deal. When we let go of our idols, we experience the thrill of real peace down deep—the kind that isn't dependent on other people, circumstances, or things. His pearls are priceless; no cheap imitations. Try it and see. I dare you to loosen your grip on the fakes and give God a chance to satisfy your soul with His Spirit, His Word, Himself. What is holding you back?

Talk with God

Meditate on these words of martyred missionary Jim Elliot: "He is no fool who gives what he cannot keep to gain what he cannot lose."[6] Turn your thoughts into a prayer, expressing your desire to let go of your idols and give God your whole heart. Write your prayer below:

> *The whole human race is foolish and has no knowledge!*
> *The craftsmen are disgraced by the idols they make,*
> *for their carefully shaped works are a fraud.*
> *These idols have no breath or power.*
>
> *Idols are worthless; they are ridiculous lies!*
> *On the day of reckoning they will all be destroyed.*
>
> *But the God of Israel is no idol!*
> *He is the Creator of everything that exists,*
> *including his people, his own special possession.*
> *The Lord of Heaven's Armies is his name!*
>
> **Jeremiah 51:17-19**

Day 3: Counterfeit Consequences

God gave His people consequences after repeatedly trying to get their attention by sending His prophets who put His laws and history before them. Yet they chose to keep making their own gods. They let the things they could touch and feel replace the real God who had created and loved them.

As we continue to look at the consequences for their idolatry, keep in mind that God was willing to stop these consequences if they would stop their idolatrous ways. Eventually, after their continual disobedience, God's patience waned and His righteous anger flared.

Read Jeremiah 7:5-34 and fill in the chart below.

Things God wanted them to stop	Consequences for their actions
vv. 5-6	v. 7 (reverse it)
v. 9	vv. 14-15
v. 18	vv. 19-20
vv. 30-31	vv. 32-34

Just as good parents can't stand to see their children make bad choices that lead to pain, God does not want His children to make choices that bring them harm. He is the perfect parent, and He clearly lays out His expectations through His Word. However, when He sees His people continually making self-destructive choices, He steps in to draw them back to the right path. He will go to any length to help them, which includes discipline.

Based on what you wrote in the chart above, summarize what God said to His people regarding their behavior and the ensuing repercussions if they did not stop:

Just as our idolatry takes a different form today, the consequences of our idolatry also take shape differently in our culture. Yesterday we identified some of the common idolatries of our culture—things such as people, hobbies, health, ideas, jobs, possessions, and habits.

How do our idolatrous distractions compare and contrast to those of Jeremiah's day?

Cultures change one person at a time. The first step in turning the tide of our nation starts with a look in the mirror. The only person I can truly change is me. As we take steps of obedience toward God and realize the ramifications of our personal idolatry, it causes a ripple effect to those in our spheres of influence. As we forsake idols and let God take first place in our lives, those around us may be inspired to make their own changes and affect those in their sphere of influence. This is where Jesus started: one person at a time.

Now let us take this one step closer to home and consider how our personal idolatry grieves and offends our God. Our idolatry grieves and offends Him so intensely because it leads us needlessly into slavery. God sent His Son to purchase our freedom at a very high cost. Watching us live enslaved to idols must be similar to loving parents watching their drug-addicted child ruin his or her life. I can only imagine the mixture of heartbreak and anger.

As I parent my four children, who are all in the tween and teen years, I often must enforce painful consequences. When my kids choose to go their own way and make choices contrary to the rules we have set for their safety and to what we believe to be best for them, I must admit I can get angry. Their disregard for siblings, their lack of trustworthiness when we discover they have lied, and their decisions that threaten their personal safety cause anger to rise up in me out of my great love for them. I desperately want them to make decisions that will lead to their ultimate protection and success. When I find out they've lied to me, it hurts and angers me in the same moment. I want to trust them, and this sets our relationship back and brings consequences into their lives.

I believe God feels heartbreak and anger when we sin, not because of His lack of love, but because He desires our good and knows how our disobedience causes setbacks in our relationship with Him. The theme of God's intense reaction to idolatry is found throughout the pages of Jeremiah.

> *As we take steps of obedience toward God and realize the ramifications of our personal idolatry, it causes a ripple effect to those in our sphere of influence.*

> *I believe God feels heartbreak and anger when we sin, not because of His lack of love, but because He desires our good and knows how our disobedience causes setbacks in our relationship with Him.*

Read the following verses and circle any words related to anger or wrath. Underline any words related to idol worship.

Listen to the weeping of my people;
*   it can be heard all across the land.*
"Has the Lord abandoned Jerusalem?" the people ask.
*   "Is her King no longer there?"*

"Oh, why have they provoked my anger with their carved idols
*   and their worthless foreign gods?" says the Lord.*
                                                    Jeremiah 8:19

"I, the Lord of Heaven's Armies, who planted this olive tree, have
ordered it destroyed. For the people of Israel and Judah have done
evil, arousing my anger by burning incense to Baal."
                                                    Jeremiah 11:17

"I will tell your enemies to take you
*   as captives to a foreign land.*
For my anger blazes like a fire
*   that will burn forever."*
                                                    Jeremiah 15:14

"The wonderful possession I have reserved for you
*   will slip from your hands.*
I will tell your enemies to take you
*   as captives to a foreign land.*
For my anger blazes like a fire
*   that will burn forever."*
                                                    Jeremiah 17:4

"Look! The Lord's anger bursts out like a storm,
*   a whirlwind that swirls down on the heads of the wicked.*
The anger of the Lord will not diminish
*   until it has finished all he has planned.*
In the days to come
*   you will understand all this very clearly."*
                                                    Jeremiah 23:19-20

"Do not provoke my anger by worshiping idols you made with your own hands. Then I will not harm you."

Jeremiah 25:6

"The sins of Israel and Judah—the sins of the people of Jerusalem, the kings, the officials, the priests, and the prophets—have stirred up my anger."

Jeremiah 32:32

"They provoked my anger with all their wickedness. They burned incense and worshiped other gods—gods that neither they nor you nor any of your ancestors had ever even known."

Jeremiah 44:3

Based on these verses, write a summary of God's reactions when we worship anything except Him:

God, Who is so loving and gracious that He sent His own Son to die for our sins, wants what is best for us. This is why He desires to be first in our lives. He does not want to play second fiddle to anything or anyone. Though it is right to emphasize God's great love and grace, we must not forget His wrath—His righteous anger toward sin. It is that anger that makes His grace so great. He poured that wrath out on Christ as a punishment for our sins. When we continue to live in idolatry, we cheapen His incredible sacrifice. He allowed His one and only Son to suffer and take this wrath on Himself. He bought our freedom at a great price. Why do we continue to choose slavery?

Over and over God tells us what makes Him angry—and rightfully so. The people of Jeremiah's day wouldn't listen. They had access to the law of Moses as well as God's messengers proclaiming His word. Yet they couldn't see God. They didn't see immediate consequences.

I too can continue in sin because it seems I am "getting away" without punishment. What I don't always realize is that even when I don't see immediate results of my personal idolatry, the apathy in my spirit, the missed opportunities, and the ultimate consequences on my relationships do affect me.

> *God ... wants us to put away our idols and worship Him, because this is what leads to our wholeness and peace.*

How have you taken your own personal idolatries too lightly? What excuses or rationalizations have you made for putting other things before God in your life?

God does not take idolatry lightly. He is jealous over our relationship with Him. Just as we love our children enough to give them consequences, so our heavenly Father is willing to discipline us. Yes, we are under the new covenant now. We have Christ's sacrifice as the payment for our sins. However, God still wants us to put away our idols and worship Him, because this is what leads to our wholeness and peace.

We can be so busy with all the details of work, family, school, sports, and hobbies that we stumble in the door at the end of the day and want to escape by turning on the TV or computer or turning to food or some other empty habit. We justify our bad habits, our consumer attitudes, our selfishness, and our idols just as the people of Israel did. Oh that we would learn our lessons without having to endure the heavy consequences as they did. The wholeness that comes from a right relationship with God is what I want for my children, and I know it is what God wants for us.

Romans 8:1 tells us "there is no condemnation for those who belong to Christ Jesus." And this is good news! Let us not forget, however, that God makes us aware of our sin and asks us to turn from it. God takes your sin and mine very seriously. It is no joke to Him. Like a good father, He desperately wants us to obey His Word. He is jealous for you because He loves you so deeply.

Has today's lesson changed your attitude about how seriously God takes our sin? If so, how?

Read Through Jeremiah:

Read Jeremiah 10.

Don't think it is too late! In Jeremiah 7:3, God said, "Even now, if you quit your evil ways, I will let you stay in your own land." In other words, He would preserve and protect them. He says the same thing to us. "Even now" we can turn away from counterfeits and run straight into His arms.

What will it look like for you to "quit your evil ways" right now?

Write the name of one person you will ask to pray for you and help hold you accountable in this area:

Talk with God

Take some time to confess sin before your loving Father right now. Admit to Him anything that brings guilt or shame in your life. Remember that Romans 8:1 says that those who follow Jesus do not receive condemnation. Lay all of these things at the feet of Jesus and know that you are forgiven and accepted through the blood of Christ.

Day 4: Resources

I'm just going to admit it. I am a Dave Ramsey junkie. My husband, Sean, calls him "the other man in my life." When I talk to Sean on the phone during the day and he hears someone in the background, he'll say, "What's Dave got to say today?" I download his podcasts, and they entertain me while I do chores around the house. I'm not sure why I'm so intrigued by the money problems and successes of the callers. What I have learned listening to the *Dave Ramsey Show* is that many of us in the United States, who have so much more than the rest of the world, don't have a clue where all the money has gone at the end of every month.

Today we are going to look into Jeremiah for "what not to do" in our attitudes and actions toward money. Just as Stacy and Clinton keep us from fashion *faux pas* on the television show *What Not to Wear*, Jeremiah cleans out the closet of money myths. Let's start with the first issue God repeated continually. He was very concerned about Judah's sins of omission.

> *Many of us in the United States, who have so much more than the rest of the world, don't have a clue where all the money has gone at the end of every month.*

Write under the stick figures the five people groups God specifically names in these three passages in Jeremiah. Some groups are named in more than one passage, so look for the new group(s) mentioned in each. The first letter of the word is provided as a clue.

5:27-29   **7:5-6**   **22:2-3**

O_____   P_____   F_____   W_____   I_____

The people were greedy and neglected those who couldn't take care of themselves. The orphans, poor, foreigners, widows, and innocents lived in poverty while the rest of the country got rich and thought only of their own luxury. We cannot take this too lightly. Serving those who cannot care for themselves is not a box to be checked off on our "Christian duty" list. It is the essence of what it means to know God.

Read Jeremiah 22:16 and write the second part of the verse below:

God is saying that how we treat others reveals something about our love for Him. If we know Him and walk closely with Him, our hearts will align with His to help those with very real, tangible needs. Our compassion will be stirred just as God's is when He hears the cries of His people.

Read James 1:27 in the margin. This verse backs up Jeremiah 22:16, giving us a definition for "true religion." What is it?

Pure and genuine religion in the sight of God the Father means caring for orphans and widows in their distress and refusing to let the world corrupt you.

James 1:27

Let's bring this closer to home. Approximately 21,000-plus children die every day across the globe of preventable diseases.[7] Lack of clean water, good nutrition, and proper medical treatment leads to this horrifying number. For the first few days after I came across this statistic, I thought about it a lot. My kids freak out when they can't have an ice cream cone, brand-name shoes, or a cell phone. We live in a First-World bubble of privilege and excess. My husband and son broke out of that bubble last year. On a trip to Guatemala they saw children so thankful for one bowl of rice a day—their only meal. Sometimes I want to live in my own little world and forget about kids who don't have enough to eat or who have worms in their feet because they have no shoes. Our Guatemalan missionary friend says that having worm-infested feet is normal to them. I want to cry every time I think about it.

We can't "fix it." Poverty is complex and widespread. So what does God want us to do? After reading Jeremiah's messages to the people, I know what God wants us *not* to do, and that's ignore it. We simply cannot continue to ignore poverty.

Although we can't solve the problem, each of us can play a role in helping others. There are so many great organizations that offer child-sponsorship opportunities, community feeding and housing programs, tutoring in low-income schools, and the list goes on. We are not called to them all, but we are called to do *something*. Proverbs 21:13 says, "Those who shut their ears to the cries of the poor / will be ignored in their own time of need." We can't just shake our heads, cover our ears, and say "La, la, la. I don't hear the cries of the poor, Lord."

> *We are called to do something. . . . We can't just shake our heads, cover our ears, and say "La, la, la. I don't hear the cries of the poor, Lord."*

Pray and ask God how you can get involved in answering the cries of the poor with your time, talents, and treasure. Look at your budget; if you are married, ask your husband to look at it with you. What sacrifice can you make (great or small) to help a child in need live a full life?

What will you do to help the poor in your community? In the world?

Jeremiah digs a little deeper and explores why the people weren't helping the poor. To help us see what God is trying to communicate to us through Jeremiah, let's look first at the story of Vicky Talbot. In 2008, she was diagnosed with a peptic ulcer, a possible ovarian cyst, and irritable bowel syndrome after many doctor visits and complaints of bloating and pain in her abdomen. Since Vicky was only twenty-five years old, the doctors didn't take her very seriously. They ran tests that showed no abnormalities and sent her home with antacid pills. By the time they realized she had bowel cancer, her tumor was the size of an orange.[8]

How would you feel if Vicky Talbot was your daughter or sister? Write below at least three emotions that you would feel about the situation:

1.

2.

3.

"From the least to the greatest, their lives are ruled by greed. From prophets to priests, they are all frauds.

They offer superficial treatments for my people's mortal wound. They give assurances of peace when there is no peace."

Jeremiah 6:13-14

"I will give their wives to others and their farms to strangers. From the least to the greatest, their lives are ruled by greed.

Yes, even my prophets and priests are like that. They are all frauds.

They offer superficial treatments for my people's mortal wound. They give assurances of peace when there is no peace."

Jeremiah 8:10-11

The doctors offered Vicky superficial treatments for what could have been fatal. Just two chapters apart, Jeremiah repeats a similar story of misdiagnosis. God doesn't want us to miss this. Lean in close spiritually.

Read Jeremiah 6:13-14 and 8:10-11 in the margin. What do you think God is trying to communicate when He says, "They offer superficial treatments for my people's mortal wound"?

In these two short passages God is saying a mouthful. He is outraged. This is one of those passages from Jeremiah that rings so true in our culture. Twice God said they were offering superficial treatments for His people's mortal wound.

"From the least to the greatest," their lives are ruled by what?

It wasn't just the kings. It wasn't just the poor. Everyone was consumed with the need for stuff. Those who had a lot wanted more. Those who had little wanted more.

How do you see greed fleshed out in the circles you run in?

We often don't see ourselves as greedy and neglecting the poor. However, when we are consumed with a desire for more—a nicer house, a better vacation, even simple things like new carpet—we can allow greed to rule our hearts. It's not about the things themselves, as we've been learning this week about idolatry; it's about the place they take in our hearts. God wants to give us good gifts but not to have those gifts take priority over Him.

> *God wants to give us good gifts but not to have those gifts take priority over Him.*

Aren't greed and the desire for "more" what our world offers as well? They tell us through commercials, billboards, movies, and TV shows that things, people, and status will make us happy. The culture presents images of fame, romance, or some new product as the answer for the ache deep in our hearts. It is a superficial treatment for the mortal wound that is our need for a relationship with God. When we settle for stuff to fulfill us, it's like putting a bandage over a bloody, gaping wound. It's a superficial treatment. Sin is the mortal wound that separates us from Him. We need Christ, not more stuff.

Now look back at what you wrote about how you would feel if Vicky Talbot was your daughter or sister. We are God's daughters, and He is hoppin' mad that we are taking antacids when cancer is growing in our souls. We need Him desperately. Christ is the only true healer of our hurt. We all have the God-shaped hole. It's a mortal wound. Putting status, athletics, appearance, pills, possessions, or even other people in there will not fix it. So when the world offers these as remedies for our mortal wound, our Daddy gets upset.

God is concerned about how we manage what He has entrusted to us. Are we offering Him our firstfruits by tithing to our church? Are we praying for those who are truly in need—whether around the corner or around the world? Are we willing to go to see with our own eyes and make the needs known to those around us? Will we cast a vision for those in our sphere of influence by our words and our example, communicating that God has given us money not only to spend on ourselves but also to use for His kingdom?

Read 1 Timothy 6:6-10 in the margin. Paul outlined for Timothy two sides of the continuum in our attitudes about money. Label them below, writing a description above each circle.

vv.6-8   vv. 9-10

Yet true godliness with contentment is itself great wealth.

After all, we brought nothing with us when we came into the world, and we can't take anything with us when we leave it.

So if we have enough food and clothing, let us be content.

But people who long to be rich fall into temptation and are trapped by many foolish and harmful desires that plunge them into ruin and destruction.

For the love of money is the root of all kinds of evil. And some people, craving money, have wandered from the true faith and pierced themselves with many sorrows.

1 Timothy 6:6-10

Now go back and write inside each circle the results or repercussions given in the passage in regard to each attitude—contentment on one side and the love of money on the other side.

We need to stop and evaluate our finances. We stop to get a coffee, pay a few bills, go to the nail salon or a movie, and then we wonder why we can't pay for car repairs when something breaks. Those of us who live in America are considered wealthy by the world's standards, yet most of us complain frequently about how expensive everything is and how we need more money—myself included. If we or our loved ones have jobs, it is God who has given us the abilities or skills needed to do the work. Everything we have has been provided to us by our Creator.

What material things have the most lure in your heart? (Be honest. You won't be asked to share.)

Read Through Jeremiah:

Read Jeremiah 11–12.

What non-necessity item would be difficult to cut from your budget in order to help others?

Are you willing to give it up if God asks you to? Write your thoughts below:

When we start from the vantage point of realizing that our possessions are entrusted to us for our use instead of being entitlements, it helps us to not be consumed with a desire for more and to give to others in need more freely.

Talk with God

Lay your personal finances before the Lord. Take some time to thank Him for His provision for you, and ask Him to give you a spirit of contentment with what you have. Think of at least two things to thank Him for today. Now ask God to give you His compassion for the poor. Pray by name for someone you know with a financial need.

Day 5: Making a Fake

Today we end our week's focus on idol worship, though idolatry will pop up sporadically in our study because the worship of counterfeits so warped the hearts and minds of the people of Judah. As we search the pages of Jeremiah to try to understand the people of Judah's fascination with fakes, we can't help but notice their tendency to create a god when God seemed silent or distant.

Envision with me the women of Judah. They might have been drawing water from the well, preparing food in an outdoor kitchen shared by neighbors, or sitting around weaving cloth or sewing clothes. They reminisced about the stories passed down by their grandmothers about Abraham, Moses, or King David and Solomon when the nation of Israel was a great kingdom. They surmised that their God must have lost His power or be weaker than the gods of Babylon, Egypt, and Assyria. Much bigger nations had become the playmakers with wealth, power, and control; so logically their gods must have been stronger. All the surrounding nations embraced many gods, making them polytheists. Judah alone still clung to its monotheism by worshiping one God—at least that was the nation's heritage.

Fun Fact:

The people of Egypt and Babylon practiced astrology as well as worshiped the sun, moon, and stars.

When the going got tough, instead of clinging to the God of their ancestors, Judah decided to make themselves some new gods. Oh, they weren't original gods. They borrowed them from many of the surrounding nations. These women decided their religion was outdated and needed a modern makeover. So what if they tweaked it a little to make it better? That's what we women are skilled at—making suggestions on how to do things better. However, when it comes to the sovereign ruler of the universe, we must dare to hope in His way over ours.

God holds nothing back about the ridiculous notion of making your own gods. Today we'll camp out in Jeremiah 10 to hear God's thoughts about making our own gods.

First, read through Jeremiah 10:1-16. Then go back through the verses as you fill out this chart to compare idols and our God.

Idols	The True God
v. 5	vv. 6-7
vv. 8-9	v. 10
v. 11	vv. 12-13
vv. 14-15	v. 16

Now sum up in one sentence the key difference between idols and God:

Exactly! Idols aren't real, and God is! That is what it really comes down to here. When we are disappointed with God because of our circumstances or His lack of intervention in our troubled lives, we are most likely to come up with our own plan instead of following His. We are tempted to manipulate and massage our situation instead of waiting for God. As we turn back the pages of Scripture to the patriarchs, we see others who tried to do this. Abraham's wife, Sarah, got tired of waiting for God to fulfill His promise of a son, so she attempted to "help" God out by giving her maidservant to sleep with her husband. It didn't turn out well. Rebekah knew that God had said that her younger son, Jacob, would be greater than the older twin, Esau. Rather than trusting in God's plan, she too tried to force the outcome God had already promised by leading Jacob to deceive his father.

How about you? How have you tried to "help" God at some time in your life, instead of trusting and waiting on Him? How did it turn out?

Now look again at Jeremiah 10:5 (in the margin). How did God describe idols in this verse?

> *"Their gods are like helpless scarecrows in a cucumber field!*
> *They cannot speak, and they need to be carried because they cannot walk.*
> *Do not be afraid of such gods, for they can neither harm you nor do you any good."*
>
> **Jeremiah 10:5**

It reminds me of my East Texas grandpa. Listen for the accent in my paraphrase: "Those idols are about as lifeless as scarecrows in a melon patch." God was comparing their idols to lifeless scarecrows that have no power—neither to help nor to harm. The fact that God mentions these scarecrows are in a melon patch—or cucumber patch, as some versions translate it—is interesting. Melons and cucumbers have something in common. They grow on the ground on a vine with leaves that camouflage them. For years I have sent my kids out to gather the cucumbers from our garden. When they were little, they said there weren't any cucumbers ready to pick. So I took them out and showed them how to investigate and look a little harder for the cucumbers hidden among the leaves and vines.

Scarecrows are lifeless, but they do scare birds away and keep them from eating crops such as berries or corn. Their value is worthless, however, in a cucumber or melon patch where the harvest is well hidden just the way God made it.

God goes to great lengths here in Jeremiah to convince us of the emptiness of our idolatry. He wants us to see Him in contrast to a useless scarecrow meant to guard crops that are already protected. While the scarecrow is lifeless and worthless, God is real and powerful. He is the Creator of life, and He is able to protect us from real threats to our souls. Too often our

God is real and powerful. He is the Creator of life, and He is able to protect us from real threats to our souls.

lack of faith keeps us trusting in scarecrows instead of the true God who has our best interests at heart.

If I really believe God is who He says He is in His Word, then I won't worry so much about my children's health. I will pray more and manipulate less. I will see my own sin and blind spots and be less focused on the shortcomings of others. Sometimes my attitudes, actions, and lack of prayer reveal that I am making my own back-ups instead of trusting fully in God's ability to care for me. Often I fashion a god that doesn't intervene, a god that's involved only in the "big" things instead of the details, a god who is waiting for me to mess up. That is my personal counterfeit god—not the true and living God. It's a scarecrow in a cucumber patch.

Our God is no lifeless scarecrow! He made the earth with His strong hand and powerful arm, and nothing is too difficult for Him.

What counterfeit characteristics of God have you allowed to creep into your thinking?

How does Jeremiah 10:1-16 expose any false ideas about God in your mind and heart?

God is no idol. Yet often we create a counterfeit god in our minds. We begin to think of God as how we perceive Him rather than how He is. We start to create in our mind what He is like instead of looking to His word for the truth about who He is. There is an amazing verse that helps clear up any misconceptions about what our God is like.

"O Sovereign Lord! You made the heavens and earth by your strong hand and powerful arm. Nothing is too hard for you!"

Jeremiah 32:17

Meditate on Jeremiah 32:17 (in the margin). Then copy the verse onto a note card or scrap of paper, and put it somewhere you will see it often.

Our God is no lifeless scarecrow! He made the earth with His strong hand and powerful arm, and *nothing* is too difficult for Him—not your marriage or family problems, your finances, your friendships, or your work or church difficulties. Not even the most difficult person in your life!

Next week we'll spend even more time learning about God's character and nature as we talk about what it means to know and listen to God. We'll see Him as an artistic potter and a military commander in chief as well as the personal God who knows every hair on our heads. He is no idol. He is the sovereign Lord who leads us to declare, "Nothing is too difficult for You!" (HCSB).

Talk with God

Spend a few minutes praising God for who He is. Write a prayer below, asking Him to give you faith to trust Him fully and to "smash" any idols that have taken His place in your life.

Read Through Jeremiah:

Read Jeremiah 13–14.

<u>Digging Deeper</u>

Who is the Queen of Heaven mentioned in Jeremiah? Was she Astarte, the daughter of the Egyptian sun god Ra, or the Babylonian goddess Ishtar? To see who this goddess might have been and how we can relate to the worship of love and power in our own lives, check out Digging Deeper Week 2: "The Queen of Heaven" at AbingdonWomen.com/Jeremiah.

Video Viewer Guide

WEEK 2: RECOGNIZING COUNTERFEITS AND THE REAL DEAL

Idolatry

We all have a _____ _____.

"Go west and look in the land of Cyprus;

    go east and search through the land of Kedar.

Has anyone ever heard of anything

    as strange as this?

Has any nation ever traded its gods for new ones,

    even though they are not gods at all?

Yet my people have exchanged their glorious God

    for worthless _____!

The heavens are shocked at such a thing

    and shrink back in horror and dismay,"

    says the LORD.

"For my people have done two evil things:

They have abandoned me—

    the _____ of living water.

And they have dug for themselves _____ _____

    that can hold no water at all!"

Jeremiah 2:10-13 NLT

VIDEO VIEWER GUIDE: WEEK 2

Dear children, keep away from anything that might take _____
_____ *in your hearts.*

1 John 5:21 NLT

God wants us to trust in Him, not in our counterfeits, because only He can

_____ our spiritual thirst.

The Spirit and the bride say, "Come." Let anyone who hears this say, "Come."
Let anyone who is thirsty come. Let anyone who desires drink freely from the
_____ *of* _____.

Revelation 22:17 NLT

We're _____ so we need to drink often.

We _____ from what we drink.

Week 3

OPENING OUR EARS

Listening

Memory Verse

"Ask me and I will tell you remarkable secrets you do not know about things to come."

Jeremiah 33:3

Day 1: Called to Listen

Fun Fact:

Jeremiah is credited by most scholars with authoring the Book of Lamentations.

I love sixth-grade girls. They are eager, silly, and never at a loss for words. In my small group of sixth-grade girls at church, we were talking about issues going on in their middle-school lives. They have problems with friends, teachers, and, of course, boys. One of the girls was telling a story in great detail about a misunderstanding with her teacher. I asked what her mom thought about the situation, because if she had all the facts straight, this parent would be one upset momma. I was shocked to find that this girl had not discussed what was going on with either her mom or dad.

I was intrigued. Of the five girls in the room, all agreed that they don't tell their parents most of what is really going on in their hearts and minds. Panic rose inside me because I have twin fifth-grade girls. *Will they stop talking to me next year?* I wondered. I pressed further. Did they think their parents would punish them? Would they overreact? Why the lack of communication?

In a small group, these girls are never a quiet bunch. However, the resounding response was something like this: "My parents don't listen; when I talk, I can see they are thinking about something else. They are busy and preoccupied, and my little school or friend problems aren't important to them. Eventually, I just quit telling them all the details because they don't listen anyway or they act like the things I'm concerned about are silly or unimportant." This composite of multiple responses alarmed me.

When I went home after leaving my sweet sixth-grade girls and sat down with my daughters to inquire about my own listening skills, I wasn't prepared for their responses. They had some similar feelings. "You're always on the computer or phone or working in the kitchen, and you seem distracted or even irritated when I try to tell you something." I have to admit, there is a lot on my mind most of the time. I don't want my girls to stop talking to me and find other ears willing to listen. Later, when they have questions about their friends, boys, and even their faith, I don't want

> *If my listening skills aren't the greatest with my own children, who are physically present and asking for my attention, how much easier is it for me to struggle with listening to my Creator God?*

to discover I've lost the opportunity because I didn't take the time to listen when they had a long, detailed story about the characters in a book they were reading or the ongoing saga of how Sally and Jennifer weren't getting along at school.

I began to wonder: if my listening skills aren't the greatest with my own children, who are physically present and asking for my attention, how much easier is it for me to struggle with listening to my Creator God? This is a question we all need to ask. Are we really listening? In studying the Book of Jeremiah, I see a resounding theme that occurs over and over: God wants His people to open their ears and listen to Him. God's repetition of this theme tells us He doesn't want us to miss this point.

Look up the following passages in the Book of Jeremiah. Every time you see the words *listen* and *ears* (or any synonym for these terms), put a tick mark beneath the corresponding word below.

	Listen	Ears
5:20-22		
6:8-12		
7:13, 24-28		
9:20		
19:15		
25:4-5		
26:3-9		
35:15-17		
44:24-25		

Did you notice that no one was exempt from the call to listen? People specifically addressed in these verses include Israel, Judah, Jerusalem, my people, priests, prophets, and even women (twice singled out). God also let them know the attempts He had made to speak to them.

What were some of the ways God tried to get through to them?

How has God spoken to you through His Word, circumstances in your life, and His messengers (this would include pastors, teachers, books, and the Bible itself)?

In all of these passages, the Hebrew word translated into English as *hearken, hear,* or *listen* is *shama*, which means "to hear with attention or interest."[1] *Shama* occurs over one thousand times in the Old Testament. You may recognize this word, which refers to what became a very important element of Judaism following the exile. It would have been familiar to the people of Judah during Jeremiah's time because the cornerstone of the monotheism that set them apart from the polytheist nations surrounding them is found in Deuteronomy 6:4, known as the Shema or Shama: "Listen, O Israel! The LORD is our God, the LORD alone."

> *The Hebrew word translated into English as* hearken, hear, *or* listen *is* shama, *which means "to hear with attention or interest." Shama occurs over one thousand times in the Old Testament.*

One source explains that "the Shema is the central prayer in the Jewish prayerbook (Siddur) and is often the first section of Scripture that a Jewish child learns. During its recitation in the synagogue, Orthodox Jews pronounce each word very carefully and cover their eyes with their right hand. Many Jews recite the Shema at least twice daily: once in the morning and once in the evening."[2]

In Jeremiah's time, the people failed to listen, and God got their attention by allowing them to be taken captive. It is interesting that during the time of Ezra when the people returned after seventy years of captivity just as Jeremiah had prophesied, the Jewish book of prayer (Siddur) first surfaced. The Shema is the central prayer perhaps because the people realized the consequences of their closed ears and wanted to be careful not to repeat their mistakes.

How do you think we are doing with *shama* **(listening to God) today? Why?**

When you think about your own spiritual ears, do you perceive them as open or closed?

Beside each of the following references to the people of Judah's closed ears found in the Book of Jeremiah, write a word or phrase that contrasts their closed ears and helps us see what open ears would look like:

CLOSED	OPEN
1. Don't want to listen (6:10)	1.
2. Refuse to answer (7:13)	2.
3. Stubborn (7:26)	3.
4. Distracted by the world's ways (35:15)	4.
5. Disobedient to God's ways (44:25)	5.

To have open ears means to listen, respond, cooperate, maintain focus, and prove with your actions that you have heard what God is saying. Would those closest to you describe you as quick to listen, responsive, cooperative, focused, and living a life that reflects the faith you claim? We, too, struggle with closed spiritual ears, don't we? Despite the gifts of God's living Word, His Spirit, His body of believers (the church), and the life of His beloved Son, we often find ourselves distracted and stubborn like the peers of Jeremiah. God is calling us to open our ears and be willing to hear.

Two short passages in the New Testament say so succinctly what Jeremiah tried in desperation to communicate. They show us that the concept of spiritual ears has not changed with the new covenant. Shama is still God's desire for us.

Read Mark 4:24-25 and Hebrews 12:25-27 in the margin. Write a one-sentence summary of their message below:

We may not have a prophet proclaiming God's message to us in the street, but God is still calling us to listen to His message. I pray that we will not be so distracted by the minutia of daily life that we fail to hear. May our ears be open to our unshakable God. He is so worthy!

Tomorrow, we'll talk more about listening so that we can better understand who our God is and how He works in our lives.

Talk with God

Think for a few minutes about your listening skills. How open are you to what God is saying to you? If you think He isn't speaking, then chances are you haven't been taking the time to listen well. The inside of our heads can be a very noisy place. Take a few quiet moments and listen. What is God saying to you through His creation? The people around you? His Spirit? Your circumstances? His Word? What other ways are you hearing Him speak? Make some notes in the margin.

Day 2: Reading with Curiosity

Curious George is one of my favorite children's book series. The man with the yellow hat is always patient with George even though George gets into so much trouble because of his curiosity. George's caregiver knows the curious monkey isn't willfully rebelling; he just wants to know and discover things about the world. While Curious George could have a few more boundaries, we could learn from him how to be more curious.

In reading Curious George books to my adorable niece Sophia, it hit me that although George's curiosity gets him in trouble, it also is the thing that usually solves the larger problem at hand. In one particular story about a puppy that gets lost, George accidently opens all the cages at a kennel. Although his curiosity initially causes chaos, the lost puppy is found through the process of rounding up the puppies, and George becomes a hero.

I believe God wants us to use the brain He has given us to question, discuss, and work through the things we don't understand. Sometimes this creates some initial chaos, but it ends up helping us work through bigger issues of faith and relationships.

Read Through Jeremiah:

Read Jeremiah 15–16.

> *God wants us to use the brain He has given us to question, discuss, and work through the things we don't understand.*

Approaching Scripture can sometimes be daunting. It was written over 1,400 years by forty different authors moved by the Holy Spirit. The prophets especially can be books we steer away from, thinking they are too difficult to understand or not relevant to our lives. One source states, "Jeremiah, it has been claimed with some justification, is the least read and least understood of all [Old Testament] books because it reveals no clear arrangement and demands so much extrabiblical, contemporary history for its understanding. Not surprising, then, while many commentaries have been written on the Book of Isaiah, Jeremiah has suffered from neglect."[3] Statements like this can cause us to turn away from books like Jeremiah. However, I believe God has a message for us in its pages.

I have found in my own life that if I approach God's Word with curiosity—with a few simple questions in mind—I am usually overwhelmed by what God has to teach me. The questions I ask myself as I read are these:

- What will I learn about God—who He is, how He interacts with people, what the verses say about His character?
- What will I learn about myself—how I approach or not approach Him, what He calls me to do or not to do, how He expresses His love to me, what keeps me from experiencing Him more fully?
- Is there anything that God is specifically saying about my current thoughts, attitudes, or actions?

Today as we delve into Jeremiah and talk about listening to and knowing God, we will look at some of the ways God reveals His own character. Approach these passages with curiosity, asking God to reveal Himself to you through His Word.

To begin, read Jeremiah 18:1-12 and make a note of everything you learn about God in these verses:

> *The clay doesn't get to choose what kind of vessel it turns out to be. It has to trust the potter's best judgment.*

The clay doesn't get to choose what kind of vessel it turns out to be. It has to trust the potter's best judgment. This is difficult for me. I want God to work things out in a way that makes sense to me. I want to pick the color, use, and shape of how I will turn out. I certainly don't want to be fired in a kiln. However, God gives us this illustration of who He is in Jeremiah to help us understand what we often forget: He is the Potter; we are the clay.

The Hebrew word used for the potter in these verses is *Yatsar*. *Strong's Concordance* defines it, "to form, fashion, frame."[4] This is the same word used in Genesis 2:7-8 for God's creation of man from clay. In Jeremiah 1:5, this same word is used to describe how God formed Jeremiah in the womb. God is telling us that He is the former, fashioner, and framer in our lives.

We need to surrender to the Potter just as the people of Judah needed to surrender to God's instrument, Babylon. God sometimes takes us through the fire to strengthen us for use in His kingdom.

> *God sometimes takes us through the fire to strengthen us for use in His kingdom.*

How have you seen difficulties strengthen you? Give an example of something you learned through a tough time in your life.

As the Potter, God sovereignly chooses what gifts and talents to give us, what family to place us in, and what circumstances to allow us to endure to develop our endurance. However, we control the consistency of our clay. Are we stiff and resistant like the stubborn people of Judah, with closed ears, or are we soft and moldable, willing to endure pressure, trimming, and fire in order to become vessels for His use?

What kind of clay are you right now? Are you soft and moldable in God's hands, or are you fighting the work He wants to do in your life because it is painful?

Not only do we see God as the Potter in Jeremiah, we also learn about His mighty power. One name is used for God more than eighty times throughout the book. It is *Lord Sabaoth*, which is used over two hundred times throughout Scripture. Depending on the version, it is translated, *the Lord of Heaven's Armies*, *the Lord Almighty*, the *Lord of Hosts*, or *the Lord of Armies*.[5] The New Living Translation uses the Lord of Heaven's Armies.

Fun Fact:

Martin Luther used the name Lord Sabaoth in the hymn "A Mighty Fortress Is Our God."

Names in biblical times revealed character. God is telling us something about Himself through the different names used for Him throughout His Word. Read what a couple of commentators have said about Lord Sabaoth:

Hosts can refer to human armies (Exodus 7:4), celestial bodies (Deuteronomy 4:19), or heavenly creatures (Joshua 5:14). This title emphasizes the Lord as sovereign over all of the powers in heaven and on earth, especially over the armies of Israel.[6]

This is the "military" name of God, for "hosts" comes from a Hebrew word that means "to wage war." The Lord is the Commander of the hosts and heaven: the stars (Isaiah 40:26; Genesis 2:1), the angels (Psalm 103:20-21), the armies of Israel (Exodus 12:41), and all who trust in Him (Psalm 46:7, 11).[7]

> *Our problems are not too big for Him. He is holy, sovereign, and able to do what He says He will do.*

The name Lord Sabaoth is used to remind us of who our God really is: the powerful Commander in Chief with all of the angels at His disposal. Our problems are not too big for Him. He is holy, sovereign, and able to do what He says He will do. If we will listen and really get to know Him as we study His Word, we will find that He is more than worthy of our complete trust and confidence.

Read just three of the passages in Jeremiah that mention God as the Lord of Heaven's Armies. What do you learn about God's character through each of these passages?

31:35-37

32:17-20

50:33-34

Do these passages that reveal the character of God encourage you to want to listen to Him more carefully? Why or why not?

Read Through Jeremiah:

Read Jeremiah 17–18.

You have access to the Commander in Chief of the whole world. I love how Jeremiah shows us the strong side of God's power as Lord Sabaoth, yet he also shows God as the artist sitting at the potter's wheel, carefully shaping us into His image. Do you want to know Him better? He wants to know you! He wants you to ask Him questions and wait in His presence for answers.

I often laugh with God at how amazingly precise He is at speaking to my struggles or answering a specific question. Just yesterday I asked Him why Jeremiah isn't written in chronological order but seems to skip all over the place. You see, I am a "go in order" kind of person. The truths God was showing me out of Jeremiah seemed consistent thematically but were scattered here and there throughout the book. It doesn't make for neat outlines or orderly compartments. Minutes later, I read Ecclesiastes 7:13 in my daily quiet time: "Accept the way God does things, / for who can straighten what he has made crooked?" God directly answered my question! This has happened to me so many times that it no longer surprises me. In fact, I have come to expect it.

I pray that as you pursue God and wrestle with Him through the ups and downs of your day-to-day life, you will begin to see direct answers as you approach Him with curiosity.

Talk with God

Take a moment to reflect on your current joys and trials. How does the fuller understanding of God as Potter and Lord of Heaven's Armies change your perspective on what you're going through right now? Talk with God about this now.

Day 3: Cling Like Underwear

Do you like loose, baggy underwear? I don't either. Underwear doesn't look or feel good unless it fits snugly. Guys may choose between boxers and briefs, but us girls like our underwear to fit. You might be wondering where this talk of underwear is going. Believe me, this Texas girl does not enjoy public conversations of private things. It doesn't take much to make me blush. However, God is the one who mentions the "unmentionables."

This week we are learning about listening to God and really knowing Him. We all talk *about* God. At church we hear the pastor talk about God. We fit God in where it is culturally acceptable. However, how close is your relationship with Him? Do you tell Him exciting news? When the world is falling apart around you, is He the one you run to for help and support? Do your calendar and bank account reveal that He is your closest friend?

Yesterday we talked about what a holy and sovereign God He is—the Potter who molds us the way He chooses and the Lord of Heaven's Armies. Yet God chooses to speak to us in ways that we can understand, even if it means using underwear as an analogy.

Read Jeremiah 13:1-11, and write verse 11 below:

> *God wants our relationship with Him to be tight, ... God wants us to be in constant, daily contact with Him.*

God wants us to cling to Him like underwear. Underwear is not only supposed to be close; it is also personal. Undergarments are personal. We don't show them to everyone. God wants our relationship with Him to be tight, or personal.

There is one more important thing about underwear. It is meant to be daily. When I fold laundry and notice one of my daughters' panty piles is lower than her sisters', I give her a reminder—you know, to change it every day, right? Likewise, God wants us to be in constant, daily contact with Him.

How are you doing in this regard? Put a check mark next to the statement that best describes where you are with Christ right now:

_____ **Distant friend I almost never talk to**

_____ **Occasional friend not inside my closest circle**

_____ **Once a close relationship that has been slowly drifting over time**

_____ **Weekly checking in with Him**

_____ **Spend time talking most days**

_____ **Close like underwear**

God wants us to know Him—and not just through ritualistic religious function. That's what was happening in Judah, and it caused their intimacy with God to be reduced to rot because they tucked closeness with Him into a dark hole. God used Jeremiah to illustrate this point with a loincloth. A loincloth, which was made of linen, was like underwear in that it was worn close to the body.

Here are some other interesting things to note as we look at Jeremiah 13:1-11:

- Priests as well as common people wore linen garments. (God wants all people to "cling" to Him—to enter into a close relationship with Him.)
- The Hebrew word for "cling" (*dabaq*) used in verse 11 is the same one used in Genesis 2:24: "a man leaves his father and mother and clings to his wife" (NRSV). It means "to cling, stick, stay close, cleave, keep close, stick to, stick with, follow closely, join to, overtake, catch."[8]
- The Euphrates River was a seven-hundred-mile journey round trip from Jerusalem. In Jeremiah's day, four months each way would be required to make the trip. The Hebrew word translated as Euphrates is *perat*. Commentators disagree as to whether the word *perat* refers to the actual Euphrates River or another location about three miles northeast of Jerusalem, which later was "generally identified with ancient Parah."[9] Whether it was three or three hundred and fifty miles, God used this illustration of underwear to speak of God's desire for intimacy with His people.

The sin that kept the people from enjoying intimacy with God was pride. They shifted their focus from God and His Word to more tangible things they could taste and touch. For them, these tangible things were idols. As they worshiped the Queen of Heaven and made idols out of wood, they slowly drifted away from the true God. Instead of staying in close relationship with God and His Word, they chose to do what they wanted. Pride crept in. Of course, this didn't happen overnight. They didn't wake up one day and decide not to worship the true God. One small choice after another caused a domino effect until they found themselves moving in a totally different direction.

The people quit listening to God even though they had prophets like Jeremiah; even though they had portions of God's Word; even though they had oral storytelling about what God had done through Noah, Abraham, Moses, and King David. Today we have an even fuller revelation of God— His complete Word. Not only that, we also have access to some of the best Bible teaching available twenty-four hours a day through the Internet,

Fun Fact:

A loincloth was a linen undergarment worn like a short skirt around the hips, reaching midway down the thighs.

Christian TV and radio, and more books and commentaries than we could read in a lifetime—all to help us know, love, and understand who God is and what He wants to do in our lives. The question is this: are we listening to the voice of God or the voices of our culture? He wants us to cling to Him like underwear. He wants us close.

Read Luke 19:41-44 in the margin. How do these words of Jesus parallel Jeremiah 13:11, 17?

> *But as he came closer to Jerusalem and saw the city ahead, he began to weep.*
>
> *"How I wish today that you of all people would understand the way to peace. But now it is too late, and peace is hidden from your eyes.*
>
> *Before long your enemies will build ramparts against your walls and encircle you and close in on you from every side.*
>
> *They will crush you into the ground, and your children with you. Your enemies will not leave a single stone in place, because you did not accept your opportunity for salvation."*
>
> **Luke 19:41-44**

God longs for us to stay in constant contact with Him. We are leaky. I can be on a mountaintop with God worshiping Him at a women's conference and a week later feel a million miles away from Him, consumed with getting the laundry done and breaking up my kids' fights. Just as we change our underwear every day, we need to renew our closeness with God every day. We need to open our ears and listen.

Our copy of God's Word shouldn't be something we search for to take to church on Sundays; it should be something we search in daily so that we can hear from Him. When we read God's Word expectantly and curiously, we want to know who He is, how He wants us to live, and what things He challenges us to be cautious about. We shouldn't just talk about God; we should talk with God about everything we are thinking and feeling. He wants to be close. Do we?

It blows my mind that the Lord of Heaven's Armies really can use even the underwear we put on every day to call us back to Him. He is all-knowing, all-powerful, and the Creator of everything I see. Yet if I'm honest, often I would rather spend hours watching TV, chatting on the phone with my sisters and friends, and surfing on social media than connecting with the God of the universe. When I say I've been so busy I haven't had time to read my Bible and pray, I know it's a lie. We all make time for what we really want to do. I know I do. In my pride, often I'd rather do what feels good in the moment than make choices that will lead

Read Through Jeremiah:

Read Jeremiah 19–20.

to intimacy with Christ. When we do choose to come before Him and listen, we are blessed beyond measure. His love and truth wash over us as He counsels, encourages, and reminds us about His great love for us.

Talk with God

Take a moment to identify at least two things that needlessly eat up time that you could spend cultivating closeness with God. Bring these things before the Lord and ask His Spirit to reveal any steps you need to take to move a step closer in your relationship with God. Write anything He speaks to you in the margin.

Day 4: The Right Voices

Every day we are bombarded by different voices. My mailbox overflows with mail from companies trying to sell me something. Catalogs, advertisements of everything from oil changes to carpet cleaning, and credit card offers abound. Then I can browse through social media or turn on the news and see others advocating strong political causes they want us to jump on the bandwagon to support. In the checkout line, messages call me to be skinny and fit so that I will feel good about myself. There's no shortage of voices in the Christian realm either. I recently saw some video clips online from a discussion between major church leaders. The dialogue mostly consisted of pastors discussing how the modern church should approach preaching, evangelism, and discipleship.

It's great to talk, debate, and work through the issues related to trying to follow God. I'm not saying the voices are all bad. I need the news and my social media friends to keep me up-to-date on things going on in the government of which I otherwise might not be aware. But how can we know that we are following the right leaders, listening to the right voices, and walking in God's truth in the many arenas of life?

We don't want to be like the people of Judah in Jeremiah's day who didn't listen to God but, instead, chose to listen to "others" with a more popular message, such as the religious priests and prophets. They called for tolerance, freedom of expression (idolatry), and permissiveness. Sound familiar? Is it possible that we are listening to the "others" of our day instead of God's true messengers? How can we know for sure? Let's go to the source of truth and consider three insights God has for us in the Book of Jeremiah related to discerning which voices we should heed.

Fun Fact:

Jeremiah spoke against false prophets more than any other Old Testament writer.

1. Consider the moral character of the messenger.

As we seek to understand how to discern the validity of a message, we must take a look at the personal integrity of the mouthpiece. Although we must be careful about judging our leaders or expecting perfection from them, we should consider if their lives reflect their own teaching. In other words, does their walk match their talk?

Read Jeremiah 23:9-16 and check off the following descriptions of false prophets and priests as you find them in the passage. (Hint: This wording is based on the New Living Translation.)

_____ Commit adultery

_____ Do evil

_____ Abuse power

_____ Are ungodly and wicked

_____ Do despicable acts in the Temple

_____ Lead people into sin

_____ Love dishonesty

_____ Encourage those who do evil

_____ Make up everything they say

> *God's heart breaks over these people who claim to speak for God but make up their own messages. . . . there is a relationship between the messenger's life and the validity of the message. They should match.*

God's heart breaks over these people who claim to speak for God but make up their own messages. As we see in the passage, there is a relationship between the messenger's life and the validity of the message. They should match. In other words, if the message is valid, it should be reflected in the messenger's life.

When we are listening to the voices of politicians, preachers, or individuals on TV, we need to evaluate their lives and see if they are in line with what we know about God and His character. As one source points out, "The prophet always stood for God's standards and called people to Him (Deuteronomy 13, esp. v. 4), and it was this that distinguished a true prophet from a false prophet (for example 1 Kings 13:18-22; Jeremiah 28)."[10]

Jesus confirmed Jeremiah's call to evaluate the life of the messenger.

Read Matthew 7:15-20 in the margin. What two examples did Jesus use to describe false prophets?

"Beware of false prophets who come disguised as harmless sheep but are really vicious wolves.

You can identify them by their fruit, that is, by the way they act. Can you pick grapes from thornbushes, or figs from thistles?

A good tree produces good fruit, and a bad tree produces bad fruit. A good tree can't produce bad fruit, and a bad tree can't produce good fruit.

So every tree that does not produce good fruit is chopped down and thrown into the fire.

Yes, just as you can identify a tree by its fruit, so you can identify people by their actions."

Matthew 7:15-20

Jesus said that false prophets are disguised as harmless sheep while beneath that veneer they are vicious wolves. He called us to look not only at what others say but also at how they act. Our judgments about others shouldn't lead us to gossip, shaming, or self-righteousness. Instead, they should cause us to make sure that those who teach us God's Word are walking in a way that matches their talk.

Everyone sins, so no one will perfectly live out God's standards; but we should not see blatant discord between a teacher's life and message. As Jesus said, a tree is "identified by its fruit" (Luke 6:44). In Week 1 we saw how Jeremiah compared the fruit tree planted by the river to the dry, stunted shrub in the desert. Jesus said we are to listen to those whose lives are characterized by good fruit.

2. Evaluate the message to see if it lines up with God's Word.

In order to identify counterfeit dollars, experts spend time studying a genuine bill. Likewise, in order to recognize error, we must continually study the truth of God's Word. This will prepare us to exercise discernment when the many voices in our life and culture present us with information.

Read Jeremiah 23:16-32, and write verse 28 below:

What is the difference between straw and grain? Complete the statements below, and then tell how they relate to the false and true prophets.

Straw is . . .

Grain is . . .

One source observes, "Dreams of the false prophets were to the word of God as chaff to wheat. Words of false prophets have no value; those of the true messengers of God are as wheat, as food for believers."[11] Straw and grain may share some common physical characteristics, but their function couldn't be more dissimilar. While straw was collected for bedding, grain was useful for nourishment. The message of the false prophets had no lasting value. It provided temporary comfort like the straw used to make beds for people and animals in that day, but it wasn't of any value to feed them. God's Word is alive and active. It may deal out severe truth at times, but wouldn't we rather hear painful truth than comforting lies?

God's Word is alive and active. It may deal out severe truth at times, but wouldn't we rather hear painful truth than comforting lies?

I find "straw" creeping into my spiritual diet at times. I need to remember Jeremiah's message when I want to numb my problems with soul "junk food" like escaping into a novel, playing online games, or zoning out in front of the TV. These things aren't inherently bad, but they are not the spiritual food God says we need in order to grow. God wants to immerse us in His truth, but we often settle for a popular, comforting message instead. Is there a nagging in your spirit about any of the voices you are allowing to speak into your soul?

On the next page, label the following voices S for straw or G for grain. If you feel something can be both, choose the description that more consistently characterizes the influence or value it holds for you. (This is a subjective exercise, so there are no right or wrong answers.)

Straw: sometimes comforting but holds no real spiritual nutritional value

Grain: consistently speaks truth that feeds your soul (whether Christian or secular—all truth is God's truth)

TV _____	Magazines _____	Talk Radio _____
Books_____	Newspapers _____	Blogs _____
Music_____	Close Friends_____	Social Media _____
Games _____	Teachers _____	Bible Studies _____
Movies _____	Pastors_____	Online Sermons ____

The point is that we are called to evaluate the many modes of information flooding our brains on any given day. An overload can desensitize us to hidden messages that do not line up with God's Word. The issue at hand is this: are you eating any grain? Or are you lying on a bed of straw with your stomach growling? The latter can make you cranky—believe me, I know from experience. What about you? Can you think of a time when you feasted on too much straw (look at the list above), and it left you feeling empty instead of full?

Speaking of lying in straw, it can also make you itchy.

How does 2 Timothy 4:3-4 (in the margin) parallel the concept of straw and grain?

Paul wrote that a time was coming when people would want to hear comforting lies with itching ears. I believe this describes our culture. We are creatures of comfort. However, God cares more about our character than our comfort.

Not long ago I was begging God to take away a situation in my life that was about as comfortable as wearing three-inch heels while running a marathon. Some personal misunderstandings between my pastor husband and some friends who attend our church put me in the middle of a complicated predicament. I had to measure every word, test my heart motives, and beg God for wisdom as I approached both sides. I wasn't always sure when to stay out of their disagreement and when God was calling me to engage in the fracture. When we avoided the subject, it felt like an elephant in the room no one was acknowledging; but I found that addressing it sometimes added fuel to the fire of conflict. As much as I hated to admit it at the time, though, I knew that this difficult situation was the very thing conforming me to God's image and growing my faith.

Fun Fact:
Jeremiah 28 is the story of Hananiah and Jeremiah. In these seventeen power-packed verses, Hananiah represents straw (comforting lies) and Jeremiah represents grain (painful yet necessary truth). This narrative illustrates the importance of standing up for painful truth rather than settling for comforting lies.

For a time is coming when people will no longer listen to sound and wholesome teaching. They will follow their own desires and will look for teachers who will tell them whatever their itching ears want to hear.

They will reject the truth and chase after myths.

2 Timothy 4:3-4

Sometimes eating grain requires discipline and perseverance. It may be painful going down, but it brings amazing growth.

Take a moment to think about grain in your life that you may be reluctant to swallow but that you know will cause spiritual growth if you'll just keep chewing on the truth and letting it fully digest. How is God using an uncomfortable situation to grow your faith today?

"Even the stork that flies across the sky knows the time of her migration, as do the turtledove, the swallow, and the crane. They all return at the proper time each year. But not my people! They do not know the LORD's laws.

"'How can you say, "We are wise because we have the word of the LORD," when your teachers have twisted it by writing lies?

These wise teachers will fall into the trap of their own foolishness, for they have rejected the word of the LORD. Are they so wise after all?"

Jeremiah 8:7-9

If God's Word is to be our measuring rod for evaluating the messages we receive, then it is important for us to consider how well we know God's Word.

Read Jeremiah 8:7-9 in the margin. What do these verses say about the people's knowledge of God's Word during this period of biblical history?

The people didn't know God's Word, so they weren't able to discern when others twisted it. We must know God's standards and take time to sift through the way others are applying those truths in today's culture. I know it can be daunting. Sixty-six books. Over forty authors. Written over 1,400 years. The original languages of the Bible were not English. Different theological positions and interpretations within the body of Christ compel us to know and understand what we believe and why. Taking the time to read, study, question, and discern the truth can seem overwhelming in the midst of doctor's appointments, soccer practice, homework, and work schedules. However, when we get to the end of our lives and stand before our heavenly Father, what will have seemed so important that we didn't have time to read and study the living book given to us by our Creator?

When I consider the hours I've spent watching TV, chattering about nothing on the phone, or reading social media posts, I know the issue is not one of not having enough time. It's about how I choose to spend my time.

What time-waster could you reduce by fifteen minutes a day in order to spend more time in God's Word?

Now, if we're going to cut something out, we need to be ready to fill that space with God's Word before a new time-waster claims its spot! We may not have prophets shouting messages from the street corners, but every day across the planet, godly men and women are teaching God's Word and making their messages available through a variety of media. You also likely have several copies of the complete revelation of God's Word in your home in different versions and formats—print, digital, or audio.

Brainstorm some creative ways that you could increase your Bible reading or listening habits. Think specifically about time spent exercising, driving in the car, folding laundry, and winding down after the kids are in bed. Write ideas in the margin.

3. Ask the right questions.

We question everything today, from where to find the best deal to the decisions made at the PTO meeting. However, when it comes to God's Word, we sometimes just recite rote prayers or fly through a passage so we can check Bible reading off our to-do list. God wants us to read His Word curiously, asking the right questions.

Read Jeremiah 23:33-40, and write verse 35 below.

What question(s) are we to ask?

Fun Fact:

Jesus asked a lot of questions. Matthew and Mark alone record more than 150 questions that Jesus asked.

Our approach to God's Word, whether it is taught by a preacher, author, or scholar—in person or in mainstream media... should be active listening rather than passive acceptance.

We have the truth. We have more than Moses and the prophets had. We have the Gospels, the letters of Paul, and more—the complete revelation of God. We need to be careful to read and listen well to what has been entrusted to us. We don't just need to have "quiet time." We must seek to understand—to read God's Word asking the Holy Spirit to give us spiritual wisdom so that we may understand and apply His truth in daily life. Our approach to God's Word, whether it is taught by a preacher, author, or scholar—in person or in mainstream media, including print resources such as this Bible study or the many others like it—should be active listening rather than passive acceptance. We should ask questions such as these:

What is being presented?
Does it line up with the whole of Scripture?
What is the historical and cultural context?
What interpretations do biblical scholars/commentaries offer?
What does it tell me about God's heart and character?
Where does this message need specific or general application in my life?

Asking the right questions is an important part of discerning truth.

In closing, let's take a minute to review Jeremiah's three guiding principles of discernment. Peek back if you need to, and then write them below in your own words:

1.

2.

3.

Read Through Jeremiah:

Read Jeremiah 21–22.

Now think about your daily routines, your time management, and the voices that speak into your life. Does anything need to change related to how or what you are listening to? Circle one:

YES   NO

If you circled YES, in what specific ways do your listening habits need to change—especially in regard to your study and understanding of God's Word?

Talk with God

Read over the three guiding principles of discernment once more and then pray Psalm 119:169: "O LORD, listen to my cry; / give me the discerning mind you promised."

Day 5: Keep Asking

Yesterday we considered three guiding principles from Jeremiah related to discernment. Today we're going to take a more in-depth look at principle #3: Asking the right questions.

My children don't have a problem with asking. As I'm writing this, my daughter just asked if she could have a freezer pop. "How many have you had today?" I countered. "Just two," was her hopeful reply. They have no lack of restraint in asking. I remember several years ago we were on our way home from a wonderful day at the zoo when we passed a waterpark, and they asked, "When can we go there?" I am trying to teach them to ask for things less often, or at least to ask for more appropriate things.

Today we'll see that God welcomes our asking. Asking means dialogue. I tell my kids that *questioning* is a good thing (within reason and when done respectfully). We should never stuff our doubts. Doubts are real. Everyone has them. What is most important is what we do with them. When we doubt, it should lead us to think, study, and ask questions. I write specific questions I have for God all the time. I write them in my Bible next to a passage I don't understand. I write them in my journal as I pray. Everything from, "Are you calling me to go serve my sister-in-law, or is that just my idea?" to "How do you want me to prioritize my to-do list today?"

Today we will see that Jeremiah asked God questions. They talked together regularly. When I was a child, I remember a kind Sunday school teacher telling me that God's phone number was 3-3-3. She was referring to Jeremiah 33:3. Let's start there today.

> *We should never stuff our doubts. Doubts are real. Everyone has them. What is most important is what we do with them.*

Write Jeremiah 33:3 in the margin.

In Jeremiah 33:3, God is pleading with us to come and ask. He offers to give us secret information about the future.

What questions do you have for God right now? They can be questions about Him or specific questions about your life and circumstances.

How has God answered questions for you in the past?

Let's look at some of Jeremiah's prayers to gain insights from how he interacted with God. Write any observations you have from the following passages. (What do these verses reveal about Jeremiah's approach, tone, questions, hope, authenticity, and so on?)

10:23-25

14:19-22

16:19-21

32:16-25

Jeremiah approaches God with confidence, rehearsing characteristics about who God is and how He behaves. He asks specific questions. He expresses his frustrations over things that don't make sense to him. He admits his own faults and asks God to correct him when he is wrong.

When I was in junior high, I was taught a simple way to pray that has stuck with me all these years. You may be familiar with this prayer method. It is ACTS: Adoration, Confession, Thanksgiving, and Supplication (to request humbly). I see these same elements in the prayers of others in the Bible who enjoyed intimacy with God.

The prayers of Daniel, King David, and Hezekiah also reflect adoring or praising God for who He is, sometimes using a specific name such as the Lord of Heaven's Armies. There are many examples in the Bible of confessing or admitting that we need correcting, because we all make mistakes. Sometimes this is individual confession and sometimes it is corporate confession. Jeremiah confesses the sin of the whole nation before God (14:20; 16:19). The Bible also reveals prayers of thankfulness, such as Mary's song when she finds out she is carrying the Messiah. We also find plenty of examples of asking God to intervene and save, such as David's psalms written when he was on the run from King Saul.

ACTS is not the only way to pray, since prayer is simply talking to God. However, a system such as this can help us. In the past my children's prayers often sounded like this: "God, thanks for the wonderful day today, and I hope we have a wonderful day tomorrow." Since teaching them ACTS, it has helped them learn to connect with God on a deeper level.

Let's look at a few New Testament passages that expound on what God was telling us about asking in Jeremiah 33:3. Circle words that describe what our posture in asking should look like. Draw an X over words that describe wrong ways to ask.

"And so I tell you, keep on asking, and you will receive what you ask for. Keep on seeking, and you will find. Keep on knocking, and the door will be opened to you."

Luke 11:9

I have not stopped thanking God for you. I pray for you constantly, asking God, the glorious Father of our Lord Jesus Christ, to give you spiritual wisdom and insight so that you might grow in your knowledge of God.

Ephesians 1:16-17

If you need wisdom, ask our generous God, and he will give it to you. He will not rebuke you for asking. But when you ask him, be sure that your faith is in God alone. Do not waver, for a person with divided loyalty is as unsettled as a wave of the sea that is blown and tossed by the wind.

James 1:5-6

You want what you don't have, so you scheme and kill to get it. You are jealous of what others have, but you can't get it, so you fight and wage war to take it away from them. Yet you don't have what you want because you don't ask God for it. And even when you ask, you don't get it because your motives are all wrong—you want only what will give you pleasure.

James 4:2-3

And we are confident that he hears us whenever we ask for anything that pleases him. And since we know he hears us when we make our requests, we also know that he will give us what we ask for.

1 John 5:14-15

According to the words you circled, what should your asking look like?

What are the prayer inhibitors that you put an X over?

We see the consistency of asking, listening, and knowing God in prayer all the way from Jeremiah through the entire span of the New Testament. This is a consistent theme. Ask, ask, and ask. Listen, listen, and listen some more!

God mostly answers my questions through His Word, but He sometimes uses other books, people, and circumstances. One time I honestly got an answer through a name written on the license plate of the car in front of me while I was questioning God at a stop light. It sounds crazy, I know, but I wholeheartedly believe it was a very direct and specific answer to my question. When God seems silent in my life, I usually find it's because I've either stopped asking questions or stopped taking the time to listen for the answers.

> *When God seems silent in my life, I usually find it's because I've either stopped asking questions or stopped taking the time to listen for the answers.*

How is your prayer life right now? Circle any words that apply:

Nonexistent	Occasional	Crisis prayer	Boring
Alive	Exciting	Neglected	Intentional
Constant	Real	Sporadic	Mostly at church
Routine	Awesome	Journal Prayers	

How would you like it to be?

What is keeping you from an "underwear-close" relationship with God in your prayer life? As we saw in the New Testament passages we read today, we need to keep on asking. Luke 11:8 in the New Living Translation talks about asking with "shameless persistence." We need to keep asking with the persistence of children when they want a treat or a favor. However, we must also examine our motives. Why do we want what we're asking for? Is it for our own pleasure? Will it truly benefit us in the long run?

Our Father God wants us to ask, but we also must learn to listen for His answers and trust that He is working for our good even when He doesn't give us what we request. As we cling to Him like underwear, we will find ourselves learning to listen to His voice and trust His answers are best. Then we can respond to God's call:

> Listen, you women, to the words of the LORD;
>   open your ears to what He has to say.
>   Jeremiah 9:20a

What is God saying to you today? Keep asking, and keep listening.

Talk with God

Take a few moments to pray ACTS: Adoration, Confession, Thanksgiving, and Supplication (Asking)—whether this is a familiar pattern or a first-time experience. Then take some time to get quiet and listen for answers to your questions. Write a sentence or two in the margin about your time alone with God.

We'll take some time in our group session this week to share about our asking/listening experiences with God.

Digging Deeper

As we turn the pages of Jeremiah, the days of his prophecy sound uncannily similar to ours. To take a deeper look at the parallels between Jeremiah's day and ours, go to AbingdonWomen.com/ Jeremiah and read Digging Deeper Week 3: "Cultural Cues."

Video Viewer Guide

WEEK 3:
OPENING OUR EARS

Jeremiah 13:11

Listening

Psalm 27:8

Jeremiah _devoured_ God's Word.

When I discovered your words, I _____ them.

They are my _____ and my heart's _____,

for I bear your name,

O LORD God of Heaven's Armies.

Jeremiah 15:16 NLT

Three questions to ask as you read God's Word:

1. What am I going to learn about _God_ ?

2. What am I going to learn about _me_ ?

3. What is God saying in my current _situation_ ?

"As a loincloth clings to a man's waist, so I created Judah and Israel to _be close to me_ to me, says the LORD. They were to be my people, my pride, my glory—an honor to my name. But they would not listen to me."

Jeremiah 13:11 NLT

What am I going to learn about God?
What am I going to learn about me?
What is God saying in my current circumstances?

VIDEO VIEWER GUIDE: WEEK 3

Three things about underwear that can help us to understand Jeremiah 13:11:

1. Underwear is _Close_ ; it fits.

2. Underwear is _intimate_ ; it's personal.

3. Underwear is _daily_ .

My heart has heard you say, "_Come_ and

talk with me."

And my heart responds, "LORD, I am _coming_ ."

Psalm 27:8 NLT

Week 4

STAYING SPIRITUALLY SENSITIVE

Heart Issues

"The human heart is the most deceitful of all things,
and desperately wicked.
Who really knows how bad it is?
But I, the LORD, search all hearts
and examine secret motives.
I give all people their due rewards,
according to what their actions deserve."

Jeremiah 17:9-10

Fun Fact:

The word heart *is used over eight hundred times in Scripture.*

Day 1: Heart Evaluation

Heart issues can be complicated. At times we struggle to understand just what is going on inside of us. God recently revealed some hardheartedness I didn't even know was there. It is painful. My heart literally hurts. My feelings can turn on a dime. One minute I am puffed up with self-righteousness, blaming others and feeling indignant about wrongs done to me, and the next I am broken and crying, wondering where I have erred in the latest blowup with a complicated relationship.

What I do know is that God is shattering some hardness in my heart. I know I have some steps to take in making up with this person whose harsh words have hurt me. I also know that my response was less than gracious. We seem to misunderstand each other often. I know Christ calls me to be kind, loving, and forgiving as He is toward me. But how can I get my heart in line with God's truth when my feelings pull me in another direction? This leads me to bring my heart before my God and ask Him to help me sort through pain and perceptions so that He can restore softness in my most vital organ. I don't want to stay hardhearted or I'll repeat the mistakes made by the people in Jeremiah's day.

I know Christ calls me to be kind, loving, and forgiving as He is toward me. But how can I get my heart in line with God's truth when my feelings pull me in another direction?

Your heart may be in a different place today. Perhaps yours is full of joy, contentment, and peace. God calls you to celebrate. Others of you may be hurting over different heart struggles. Perhaps your marriage is ending, your children are struggling, or someone you love is dying. No matter what our heart issues are right now,

> *Many of us have done this for years—especially in relationships with family and friends. We stuff our pain and continue living our lives without dealing with it and give resentment a chance to grow.*

we must be careful to allow God full access to our hearts. Glossing over issues, skipping to the next thing, and moving on in life without dealing with our hearts is much simpler than going through the softening process.

Many of us have done this for years—especially in relationships with family and friends. We stuff our pain and continue living our lives without dealing with it and give resentment a chance to grow. This week we are going to see the danger of allowing our hearts to get hard and the painful shattering process needed to restore them. The great news is that when we allow God to do the deep work, it fosters closeness with Him in the midst of our brokenness that is unbelievably worth it.

As we look into Jeremiah's proclamations from God to the people of Israel, we find some truths and cautions to heed about the condition of our hearts.

Read each verse and complete the following caution statements with your own words:

Jeremiah 2:35   Be careful not to say _____

_____.

Jeremiah 5:3   Be careful not to make your face _____

_____ and refuse to _____.

Jeremiah 8:6   Be careful to ask _____

and not be like a horse _____

_____.

Jeremiah 44:9-10 Be careful to humble_____,

show_____,

and follow _____.

Sometimes we need to be more careful about what we do and do not do with our hearts. Without intentional evaluation, our hearts may have become hard without our awareness until one day we find ourselves much like the people of Judah.

Think about your own heart. If God were to write two specific "be careful" statements for your heart, what might they be?

_____ (your name),

be careful not to _____,

and be careful to _____.

The Israelites were disciplined by the Lord because they claimed they hadn't sinned and they refused to say they were sorry. Jeremiah 17:1 relates these actions to the condition of their hearts: "The sin of Judah / is inscribed with an iron chisel— / engraved with a diamond point on their stony hearts / and on the corners of their altars." God found their hearts hardened like stone tablets. Stones are hard, rough, and not easily moved. Their hearts didn't get that way overnight. Gradually, they made secret choices to self-protect, blame others for their problems, and refuse to acknowledge their own errors.

I wish I couldn't relate. Yet in my own relationships there are times when I build a wall of stone around my heart because I feel I've been wronged. As a pastor's wife, sometimes it's easier not to let people get too close. When you're in ministry and your friends are part of your church family, there are lonely times when you can't share your burdens with those friends in order to keep confidentiality and to guard against gossip. The more you risk in relationships, the more you have to lose. When you get burned a few times, it can be discouraging to keep putting yourself out there.

> *The more you risk in relationships, the more you have to lose. When you get burned a few times, it can be discouraging to keep putting yourself out there.*

How about you? Draw a picture of your heart below, adding some walls around it that reflect your current state. Are your walls a welcoming picket fence or a thick stone with "no trespassing" signs posted?

Later this week we'll talk more about guarding our hearts; today our focus is on spiritual heart evaluation. We can't change the hearts of others, so we need to put down our microscopes and pick up our own heart mirrors.

Jeremiah 17:9 is one of the most often quoted verses about the heart in Scripture. Write it below:

These words of Jeremiah find confirmation in Proverbs 20:9: "Who can say, 'I have cleansed my heart; / I am pure and free from sin'?" Similarly, 1 John 1:10 tells us, "If we claim we have not sinned, we are calling God a liar and showing that his word has no place in our hearts." There is always something for God to work on in our hearts. We are never completely blameless in any conflict. We can't fix others, but we can evaluate our own hearts and repent.

When it comes to evaluating our hearts, a helpful first step is asking questions: Lord, why do I feel so sad, distracted, or empty? Why did that person's words or actions cut me so deeply? Why do I want to stay mad at my husband or friend? What part of my heart has grown hard, and what will it take to soften it again? Other questions may come to mind as you evaluate your own heart response in the situation you are currently battling. Asking questions and taking the time to understand our feelings begins the process of allowing God to do His transforming work in our hearts. If we don't acknowledge the hurt or the hate, we can't move on to the healing.

> *Asking questions and taking the time to understand our feelings begins the process of allowing God to do His transforming work in our hearts. If we don't acknowledge the hurt or the hate, we can't move on to the healing.*

A heart surgeon must first discover the source of a problem—blockages, leaky valves, circuitry issues, or any number of potential problems. So we must also identify the root of our heartaches so that we can surrender our hearts fully to the Great Physician to do some spiritual heart surgery.

Most of us spend much more time evaluating the hearts of others than we do our own. In fact, we're experts at it. We read into every word, expression, and body language cue to form a conclusion about how the other person feels and thinks and may be off course. With other people's parenting, finances, and even their marriages, we are quick to see where they are wrong. However, we should be devoting greater energy to looking at our own hearts.

Focusing on others' heart issues wastes time and distracts us from dealing with our own heart symptoms. When we spend our mental and emotional energy allowing God to evaluate the sin in our hearts first, we usually find that we see others and their situations differently. By being aware of our personal tendencies toward sin and expending our time and energy on our own repentance, we can view others with more grace and less judgment.

We should be asking God to help us understand our feelings, seeking wise counsel to help us draw out our heart issues (Proverbs 20:5), and repenting and confessing to our loving Father the wickedness hidden in our hearts. He already knows what's in them and wants us to acknowledge it so that He can renew and transform us. He offers us new hearts, but we must first surrender our sinful ones to Him.

> *Though good advice lies deep within the heart,*
> *a person with understanding will draw it out.*
>
> **Proverbs 20:5**

Write below what God says in Jeremiah 17:10:

Tomorrow we will talk about the correlation of our hearts and our actions. For now, let's put into practice today's focus on evaluating our hearts. God says He searches and examines our secret motives, so let's ask Him to show us where our hearts have begun to harden—even though it might be painful.

The condition of the human heart is seen in God's Word from Genesis to Revelation. Read over the words below that are used in Scripture to describe the heart (Scripture references are provided for further study, if desired). Read each grouping, and put a check beside any that you can relate to right now—even if you relate to only one word in the group. Check as many as resonate with your personal heart climate.

_____ **Bitter (Psalm 73:21; Proverbs 14:10)**
        Carrying the insults of others (Psalm 89:50)

_____ **Broken (Genesis 6:6; Psalm 42:4; 69:20)**
        Sick (Job 23:16; Psalm 102:4; Isaiah 1:5)

_____ Confident (Psalm 57:7; 108:1)

_____ Deceived (Deuteronomy 11:16)
Lying (Jeremiah 14:14)
Dull and stupid (Psalm 119:70)

_____ Evil, wicked (Psalm 28:3; Proverbs 26:23)
Perverted (Proverbs 6:14)
Crooked (Proverbs 11:20)

_____ Faithful (1 Kings 15:14)
True and right (Psalm 7:10; 97:11)

_____ Fearful (Joshua 2:11)
Anguished (Psalm 38:8)

_____ Fickle (Hosea 10:2)
Hypocritical (Matthew 23:28)
Filled with doubt (Luke 24:38)

_____ Fully committed to God (2 Chronicles 16:9; Psalm 125:4)
Undivided (2 Chronicles 19:9; Ezekiel 11:19)

_____ Generous (Exodus 35:5)

_____ Hard (Exodus 4:21; too many references to list)
Stubborn (Exodus 7:3)

_____ Heavy (Proverbs 14:13; Isaiah 24:16)
Full of pain (Psalm 109:22)

_____ Hateful (Leviticus 19:17)
Cursing God (Job 1:5)

_____ Loving (Deuteronomy 6:5)
Understanding (1 Kings 3:9; Proverbs 14:33)
Compassionate (Luke 7:13)

_____ New (1 Samuel 10:9)
Believing (Romans 10:9-10)

_____ Overwhelmed (Psalm 61:2)
Like wax, melting within me (Psalm 22:14)

_____ Peaceful (Proverbs 14:30; John 14:27)
Thankful (Colossians 3:16)

_____ Prayerful (Genesis 24:45; Psalm 119:145)
Searching (Deuteronomy 4:29)

_____ Proud (Proverbs 21:4; Ezekiel 28:17)

_____ Rejoicing (1 Samuel 2:1)
Glad (Psalm 16:9)
Happy, cheerful (Proverbs 15:15; 17:22)

_____ Repentant (Psalm 51:17; Isaiah 57:15)
Humble and contrite (Isaiah 66:2)
Gentle (Matthew 11:29)

_____ Sad (Psalm 13:2; 42:5)
Troubled and restless (Job 30:27)

_____ Seeking God (1 Chronicles 22:19)

_____ Sincere (Psalm 15:2
Honest (Psalm 36:10)
Pure (Psalm 24:4; 73:1)
Clean (Psalm 51:10)

_____ Turned away from the Lord (1 Kings 11:9; Psalm 95:10;
Jeremiah 17:5)

_____ Virtuous (Psalm 94:15)

_____ Willing (Exodus 35:22; 2 Chronicles 29:31)
Able to change (Deuteronomy 10:16)
Responsive (Ezekiel 36:26)
Open (2 Corinthians 6:11)

Now, using words or phrases from the list above, describe your heart attitude right now toward the following (skip any that do not apply to you):

Your husband or significant other:

Your children:

Your extended family:

Your coworkers:

Your friends:

Women in your church:

Your Savior:

God cares more about the condition of our hearts than almost anything else. Jesus said in Luke 6:45b, "What you say flows from what is in your heart." As we end today, let's glimpse at a few passages from Scripture that remind us just how important our hearts are to God.

For the following passages, draw a heart around the word *heart*, underline the who, and circle the verb related to the heart. I've done the first one for you.

For we speak as messengers approved by God to be entrusted with the Good News. Our purpose is to please God, not people. He alone examines the motives of our hearts.

1 Thessalonians 2:4

But the L<small>ORD</small> said to Samuel, "Don't judge by his appearance or height, for I have rejected him. The L<small>ORD</small> doesn't see things the way you see them. People judge by outward appearance, but the L<small>ORD</small> looks at the heart."

1 Samuel 16:7

O my people, trust in him at all times.

Pour out your heart to him,

for God is our refuge.

Psalm 62:8

We serve a God who not only looks at our hearts but also wants us to pour out our hearts to Him. He invites us to get real about our joys and pains. We don't have to hide in shame; we can acknowledge our feelings and know that He wants to help us down the path of self-discovery that leads to healing.

Talk with God

Write Psalm 139:23-24 in the margin and then take some time to wait in God's presence, asking Him to search your heart and help you see where change is needed. I pray this is a time of conviction, confession, and repentance. Seeing our hearts the way God sees them is our first step in keeping our hearts soft.

Read Through Jeremiah:

Read Jeremiah 25–26.

> *We serve a God who not only looks at our hearts but also wants us to pour out our hearts to Him.*

Day 2: Behavior Modification vs. Heart Change

After taking some time to evaluate our hearts, our tendency is to go into "change my behavior mode." We say to ourselves, "Okay, now that I see the hardness, bitterness, and deception in my heart, I will get up every day and do my quiet time, go to church every Sunday (even when I'm tired), and try to watch less TV. That should help change my heart." However, when we overconcentrate on actions, we end up like the Pharisees in the New Testament who followed rules meticulously but had hearts filled with wrong motives. It was to them that Jesus quoted the prophet Isaiah: "These people honor me with their lips, / but their hearts are far from me" (Matthew 15:8).

We find a similar statement in Jeremiah 12:2b. Write it below:

Heart change happens internally first and then displays itself externally as we acknowledge and respond to the sin we've identified.

When we look into our hearts deeply and see the deceitfulness, self-preservation, and selfishness there, we need to be careful not to try to fix ourselves. It can be a danger to become like the Pharisees and try to follow rules in an attempt to clean up our hearts. That is not what God has in mind. Heart change happens internally first and then displays itself externally as we acknowledge and respond to the sin we've identified.

In Jeremiah 3:12-25, God calls His people to take some steps once they've evaluated their hearts and found them hardened by sin. He calls them to *know it*, *share it*, and *own it* in regard to their sin. This message, which is clearly laid out in this passage, is found throughout Scripture. Let's take a look at each part of the message.

Know It

Sometimes it can be scary to admit how we feel. At times I get angry at my children, am reluctant to forgive my husband, or feel jealous of my friends. I would rather pretend that I am naturally kind, forgiving, and content; but in reality my heart "default" usually starts me in the opposite direction. In order to become more like Christ, I first must be honest about the struggle. Because God promises to be merciful, we can abandon our pride and come clean about our tendency to sin. When we evaluate our hearts, we then have the choice to ignore our heart tendencies or admit them. Being honest with ourselves is a necessary first step.

Only acknowledge your guilt. Admit that you rebelled against the LORD your God and committed adultery against him by worshiping idols under every green tree.

Jeremiah 3:13a

Read Jeremiah 3:13a in the margin. What does this verse say we need to do?

Share It

After we acknowledge to ourselves the sin in our hearts, then we move on to sharing the truth with God and others. Of course, God already knows our sin; He asks us to share it with Him for the sake of our relationship.

When our children come to us with the story of something that has happened, we listen to hear their perspective, even if we have observed with our own eyes everything they have done. This allows us to experience the event together, whether we are celebrating or mourning. In the same way, sharing our joys and pains with God brings us closer to Him.

Read Jeremiah 3:13b in the margin. What is the second thing we are to do?

Confess that you refused to listen to my voice.
I, the Lord, have spoken!

Jeremiah 3:13b

Some translations use the word "obey" and some "confess." The original Hebrew word used here is *shama*. As we talked about last week, *shama* usually means to "hear with attention or interest," but it also can mean "to cause to hear, tell, proclaim; to make proclamation."[1] Most times in Jeremiah *shama* is translated "hear" or "listen," but in this passage it is often translated "obey" or "confess." Once we know our sin, we need to confess it to God and possibly others if our heart attitudes have caused them pain.

Though we always should confess our sin to God, the decision to share with others must be led by the Holy Spirit. Sometimes our sin is between us and God alone. Perhaps others are not directly impacted or the situation does not require an outward confession. Other times we need to go and repent to those impacted by our sin. Matthew 18 gives instructions for approaching each other and giving an opportunity for confession. As we seek God's guidance, the Holy Spirit gives us clarity about whether we need to confess to God alone or to both God and others.

I had the opportunity to do this recently. It was a humbling experience. Just as Job's friends made assumptions about his guilt, I did a similar thing by taking out my "microscope" to examine another person's motives. Regrettably, I also discussed the situation with her in a public place in front of our children. Not a good idea. I was defensive and said things that couldn't be retracted. Like a tube of toothpaste, I squeezed the words out, and there was no way to stuff them back in. It took some time to work through my emotions and justifications, but after I was able to evaluate my own heart from God's perspective and see my sin, He called

me to go to her. I repented of my poor decisions and apologized for hurting her with my words and actions. Sharing my heart of ownership and regret brought us closer and took us down a path of reconciliation.

God wants us to be honest about the hardness in our hearts—with Him and with others—so that He can create newness there. Just as we must admit our symptoms to a doctor, who then can prescribe the right treatment, so we must admit our heart troubles to the Great Physician, who knows the cure. Only then are we in a position to follow His treatment of repentance and confession.

Can you think of a time when you had to confess your sin to someone you hurt? How hard was it to do? How did your confession affect the relationship?

> *God wants us to be honest about the hardness in our hearts—with Him and with others—so that He can create newness there.*

I don't know about you, but confessing my sin to others ranks low on my favorite activities list. For me, it's right up there with trips to the gynecologist, cleaning the toilets, and changing dirty diapers. I often dread it even though I know it needs to be done. It can be humbling if not downright humiliating. Confessing our sin exposes our deceitful hearts. However, James 5:16 tells us a great benefit of sharing it.

Read James 5:16 in the margin. What does it say can happen when we confess our sins to each other?

> *Confess your sins to each other and pray for each other so that you may be healed. The earnest prayer of a righteous person has great power and produces wonderful results.*
>
> **James 5:16**

In the body of Christ, we miss out on this healing too often. Many of us walk around "bleeding" from the wounds of our fellow believers. God wants to heal our relational strife, but we must be willing to humbly confess our part.

You may be saying, "But I did nothing wrong. I am the offended party. The other person needs to come and confess to me." There are times when we have been mistreated and we truly are innocent victims, such as in cases of abuse. This is not what I am talking about here. Those situations require no repentance on our part but instead the healing work of God in our hearts through forgiveness. In all other instances of relational strife, we must be willing to admit and confess our sin.

The people of Judah were unwilling to humbly confess their sin. They had a self-righteous posture, believing they had done nothing wrong. I have been there in my thinking as well when relational friction has occurred. Not only is this kind of self-deception dangerous to ourselves; it often leads us to strike back. When someone hurts us, it is the nature of our deceitful hearts to want to hurt back, whether overtly or covertly. To retaliate, we might judge, gossip, ignore, or build up high walls that say "keep out" to those who have hurt us. In one way or another, we often end up sinning. Even if the other person has 90 percent to confess and we have only 10 percent, we can share that 10 percent and humbly ask for forgiveness.

> *When someone hurts us, it is the nature of our deceitful hearts to want to hurt back, whether overtly or covertly.*

Is there anyone the Holy Spirit is bringing to mind that you need to confess sin to, so that healing can begin? (It may be sin the other person doesn't even know you've been harboring in your heart.) If this person is local, no texting, e-mail, or phone calls allowed; it must be face to face. Write below the person's name, a deadline for setting up the meeting, and any action steps the Holy Spirit is leading you to take.

Person I need to contact:

I will set up a meeting ____ today, ____ this week, _____ by the end of the month.

Action Steps:

Own It

Let's look back at Jeremiah 3:12-25 to find the next step we are to take after knowing and sharing our sin. Once we have admitted our sin to ourselves and confessed our sin to God and/or others, we then must take personal responsibility for our actions.

Read Jeremiah 3:25 in the margin. What does this verse tell us to do?

> *"Let us now lie down in shame and cover ourselves with dishonor, for we and our ancestors have sinned against the Lord our God. From our childhood to this day we have never obeyed him."*
>
> **Jeremiah 3:25**

We will expound on the idea of personal responsibility in Week 5 when we see the people of Judah blaming others instead of taking responsibility for their sin. Consider this a sneak peek. When it comes to our sin, we must "own it." When you approach the brother or sister in Christ that you named above, be sure that you own your sin. Don't say, "The devil made me do it," give three reasons why your sin was justified, or point out their own failings. That is blaming, not taking personal responsibility.

Blame is an epidemic in our culture. It's much easier to pass the buck or create excuses to validate bad decisions. God says it's better to just own it. No excuses. No blaming. Just say, "I thought/said/did this, and I am sorry."

> *Owning our sin takes us to a place of freedom because we know that Jesus has already paid the price for it.*

Taking personal responsibility for sin should not trap us in a cycle of shame or self-deprecation. Instead, owning our sin takes us to a place of freedom because we know that Jesus has already paid the price for it. He lifts our shame when we admit our sin and give it to Him. First John 1:9 assures us of this truth: "But if we confess our sins to him, he is faithful and just to forgive us our sins and to cleanse us from all wickedness." Confession is the path to healing, not condemnation.

Recall a time when you played the "blame game." Why were you unwilling or reluctant to take responsibility for your actions?

How might things have been different if you had been willing to "own it"?

What we see in Jeremiah 3:25 is a call to own it—not to remain in shame and reproach but to allow godly sorrow to move us to repentance. Only then can we revel in our God who forgives and heals. Rather than viewing God as a shame-giver in this text, focus on His character as a merciful Father who grieves to watch His children running down a destructive road. God does not want us to feel bad about ourselves but to feel grief over our destructive choices and behaviors. He wants us to acknowledge our guilt because He knows that this is the path to forgiveness, freedom, and life.

Before we leave Jeremiah 3:12-25, read through the entire passage and make a few notes below about God's character qualities revealed there. Be sure to look for His Father's heart:

This passage uses the Hebrew word *Chaciyd* (also *Chasid, Hasid*) in referring to God. It is a term that means "faithful, kind, godly, holy one, saint, pious."[2] "For I am merciful," says the Lord (3:12). The Old Testament gets a bad reputation for portraying God as militant and full of judgment. Yet what we see here is the God who is the same yesterday, today, and forever. He may go to great lengths to bring us back to Him in ways we can't always understand, but His mercy is always present. We can know, share, and own our sin because God in His mercy will forgive and help us turn from it. He doesn't ask us to clean ourselves up, fix our bad behavior, and then approach Him. He welcomes us in our brokenness. He alone can change our hearts.

Jeremiah continues the discussion of hearts in Chapter 4.

Look up Jeremiah 4:3-22 in the New Living Translation. Note six references to the word heart and any insights into the heart you glean from the verses indicated. I've done the first one for you.

1. **Verse 3:** **Hearts can get hard and need to be plowed up; good seeds can't be planted when the soil of our hearts is thorny.**

2. Verse 4:

3. Verse 8:

4. Verse 14:

Hasidic Jews derive their name from the Hebrew word Hasid *(also* Chaciyd, Chasid)*, which is used in Jeremiah 3:12 to highlight God's mercy and kindness.*

5. Verse 18:

6. Verse 19:

In verse 4, the people are told to surrender two things. What are they?

In Week 1 we talked about Jeremiah's message of surrender. Here it is again. We have to hand over the pride and power in our hearts, yielding them to God. Changing our hearts doesn't mean deciding to change our actions in our own strength. If we try that, we will fail every time. I know; I've tried. We have to come to God in our weakness and surrender because we are at the end of ourselves. That's when God's power works best. The apostle Paul wrote about this.

> *Each time he said, "My grace is all you need. My power works best in weakness." So now I am glad to boast about my weaknesses, so that the power of Christ can work through me.*
>
> *That's why I take pleasure in my weaknesses, and in the insults, hardships, persecutions, and troubles that I suffer for Christ. For when I am weak, then I am strong.*
>
> **2 Corinthians 12:9-10**

Read 2 Corinthians 12:9-10 in the margin. When Paul asked God to take His weakness away, how did God answer him?

King David is a great example of someone who understood surrender and chose to *know it, share it,* and *own it* in regard to his sin. He is called a man after God's heart because he understood that only God could help him with his sin problem. This is his prayer in Psalm 51:9-10: "Don't keep looking at my sins. / Remove the stain of my guilt. / Create in me a clean heart, O God. / Renew a loyal spirit within me."

David didn't say, "God, I know I've done wrong. So here is my plan to do everything right from now on." He recognized his inability to fix his own heart through behavior modification and his need to surrender.

We can't try to do in our human strength the work that God alone can do. We must surrender our pride and yield to God so that He can change our hearts. Even in our worst moments—those times when we have yielded to the same temptation yet again—He calls us to come. Our tendency to hide in shame started back in the garden with the very first sin, yet God still seeks us out. He never forces us to follow but waits and calls to us, offering mercy and hope. We simply have to run into His outstretched arms—knowing, sharing, and owning how very much we need Him.

Talk with God

Spend some time in God's presence right now. Flip back to yesterday's lesson where you evaluated your heart in several areas. Now write a prayer below, acknowledging your need for God to create a new heart within you toward Him and others.

Fun Fact:
King David described his heart feeling "like wax, melting within me" in Psalm 22:14.

Day 3: Where Do Broken Hearts Go?

Hearts are fragile. In the physical realm, heart disease is the leading cause of death for men and women in America. Blood pressure, blockages, attacks, aneurysms, leaking valves, irregular beats, and angina are just a few of the terms describing things that can go wrong with our hearts. In the spiritual realm, the list is even longer for the potential problems with our hearts. As I looked through the hundreds of verses in Scripture that use the word *heart*, I saw many descriptions of hearts that were sick, broken, wounded by the insults of others, anguished, troubled, and so forth.

Today as we look into the pages of Jeremiah, we find a prophecy of what lies ahead for the people of Judah. It's not a pretty picture.

Read Jeremiah 6:22-25 in the margin and write below the trials described:

This is what the Lord says:
"Look! A great army coming
from the north!
A great nation is rising against
you from far-off lands.

They are armed with bows and spears.
They are cruel and show no mercy
They sound like a roaring sea
as they ride forward on horses.
They are coming in battle formation,
planning to destroy you,
beautiful Jerusalem.

We have heard reports
about the enemy,
and we wring our hands in fright.
Pangs of anguish have gripped us,
like those of a woman in labor.

Don't go out to the fields!
Don't travel on the roads!
The enemy's sword is everywhere
and terrorizes us at every turn!

Jeremiah 6:22-25

In verse 24 we find fear and anguish compared to that of a woman in labor. If you've given birth, describe your labor experience. If you haven't, write any fears you might have from what you've heard or seen about the labor and delivery process:

Finding out I was having twins just ten days before I had them caused great fear in this gal who'd already experienced the birth of a singleton. I knew what to expect. The thought of doubling that encounter freaked me right out. Sometimes our trials are not physical experiences, such as birthing a child, but are emotional, mental, and spiritual labors. Such trials are able to birth great intimacy with Christ, but the process can be excruciating.

What are some of your current disappointments, frustrations, or problems? List them below:

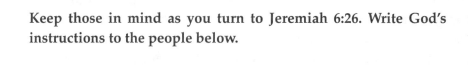

Keep those in mind as you turn to Jeremiah 6:26. Write God's instructions to the people below.

God says to mourn like the loss of an only son. He knew even then that He would be offering up Jesus as a sacrifice. Anguish and pain are not foreign to our God. He designed our frame and knows we need to express our emotions when we are hurting instead of bottling them up like our Western "grin and bear it" culture encourages. Eastern culture diametrically opposes Western practices when it comes to grieving. In biblical times, they even hired mourners when someone died, as we see in the Gospels when Jesus was called in to heal.

Today in the West we live like ducks on the water—looking cool and collected above the water line while underneath it's paddle, paddle, paddle. Sometimes the strength of the current causes us to paddle like crazy, and it seems we aren't getting anywhere. Life is hard. We often find ourselves with spiritual chest pain. Friends betray us. Our children speak hurtful words. Coworkers treat us badly. Relationships wound us. Then there are circumstances that cause us pain. We lose our jobs. Finances are tight. Divorce papers are filed. Jesus warned us it would be this way in John 16:33: "I have told you all this so that you may have peace in me. Here on earth you will have many trials and sorrows. But take heart, because I have overcome the world."

We know that Jesus is the Overcomer, yet why do we bring Him our broken hearts only after we've tried everything else to fix them? We call a friend or sister. We try to manage and manipulate the circumstances. We numb ourselves with a quick fix—food, shopping, television.

> *We know that Jesus is the Overcomer, yet why do we bring Him our broken hearts only after we've tried everything else to fix them?*

God wants us to be careful to bring our hurting hearts to Him. The Israelites had tough circumstances. They were facing invasions, poverty, and deportation from the only home they'd ever known. Instead of turning to the Lord of Heaven's Armies, they tried idol worship, political negotiations, and anything else they could think of. They lacked faith in His power to really do something.

What is the first thing you do when you are upset about something? Where do you turn?

God calls us to be careful to bring our hurting hearts to Him. Only He can heal us and use our pain and sorrow to refine us. Let's finish Jeremiah 6 to see just how God can use our trials to purify us—if we will

> *"Jeremiah, I have made you a tester of metals, that you may determine the quality of my people.*
>
> *They are the worst kind of rebel, full of slander. They are as hard as bronze and iron, and they lead others into corruption.*
>
> *The bellows fiercely fan the flames to burn out the corruption. But it does not purify them, for the wickedness remains.*
>
> *I will label them 'Rejected Silver,' for I, the Lord, am discarding them."*
>
> Jeremiah 6:27-30

yield to the process. Unfortunately, Judah had a stubborn streak for idolatry and independence that didn't fare well in the fire.

Read Jeremiah 6:27-30 in the margin. Why did God say He was putting them through fiery trials? Check any that apply:

_____ To retaliate against them for sin

_____ To burn out corruption (purify them)

_____ To determine the quality of His people

_____ To burn them up and start over with a new nation

The middle two answers are found in verses 27 and 29. God called Jeremiah a tester of metals. I'm a tea drinker, so every morning I pour boiling water over a bag of tea. The tiny leaves inside that bag permeate the water, staining it dark brown and flavoring it. Similarly, who we really are inside comes out when the "hot water" of life scalds us. Using Jeremiah's illustration, our quality of metal is revealed through the fire.

We need to be daring with hope in God rather than turning to other things to numb our pain. If we will bring it to Christ first, He can use it to refine and shape us so that we don't become like discarded, rejected silver. This illustration is not unique to the prophet Jeremiah in Scripture.

Read each of the following Scriptures and summarize in one sentence what you learn from each about fire and trials:

Mark 9:49

1 Corinthians 3:12-15

1 Peter 1:7

Based on these passages, how do you think God wants to use your current trials to refine you?

God wants us to allow Him to do a deep work in us by developing our character through difficulties. However, He doesn't force our hands. The people of Judah chose rebellion and wickedness. They fleshed out the words of Proverbs 24:10, "If you fail under pressure, / your strength is too small." Their problems made their hearts harder until seventy years of captivity finally convinced them to submit to God's ways.

How about you? Are you learning from your trials, or are you giving yourself permission to gossip, slander, and lead others into sin because of your pain? What comes out when the hot water of life is poured over you?

Read Through Jeremiah:

Read Jeremiah 29–30.

> "His [Jeremiah's] overarching concern at all times was the condition of the individual heart."[3]

In this world we will have trouble. We need to bring our troubles to the One who has overcome this world. That is our great God. God doesn't want us to ignore our problems, stuff our feelings, or pretend we aren't hurting. God wants us to come to Him, cling to Him like underwear, and trust Him even when we can't see Him and our lives seem to be falling apart. This is what it means to dare to hope in an unstable world.

Talk with God

Go to God right now with your heart burdens. Trust Him with your broken heart. Never forget how much God cares!

Here are two of my favorite verses to cling to when I am brokenhearted:

You keep track of all my sorrows.
You have collected all my tears in your bottle.
You have recorded each one in your book.

Psalm 56:8

"Then call on me when you are in trouble,
and I will rescue you,
and you will give me glory."

Psalm 50:15

If you have a verse that you cling to when you are struggling, write it in the margin. Be ready to share it with the group. If you don't, leave this space empty to write a verse someone else may share that resonates with you.

Day 4: Guard Your Heart

A dear friend called the other day to tell me about an encounter she had with her fourteen-year-old son. They were camping for the weekend, and she woke up one morning with a vivid memory of her dream. In the dream the family was driving in their van, and her son used some foul language. No one corrected him or showed any surprise at his inappropriate words. They all just went on with conversation as usual. She heard God's Spirit speak to her that her son was losing his shock factor. His exposure to bad language through school and sports was starting to desensitize him. She hadn't heard him use these words, but it was clear they needed to have a talk.

As they were driving home from camping, she had her other children ride with their father so she could have some time alone with her son. She told him, "I know you're struggling with bad language." His eyes looked like they were about to pop out of his skull. "How did you know?" he responded. "God told me in a dream," she said. His eyes were popping out even farther now. My friend took a few minutes to explain what happens when we don't guard our hearts. We lose our shock factor. She explained that it's like when a frog is put into a pot of lukewarm water and the heat is slowly turned up. The frog won't jump out even when the water boils because the temperature slowly creeps up on him until it's too late. She encouraged her son not to let this happen with his words.

I told my own kids this story so that they would know that even if I don't catch them, God can use other ways to help me parent them!

The Israelites in Jeremiah's day had also lost their shock factor. Jeremiah repeats a word picture over and over to describe their condition.

Look up Jeremiah 6:15 and 8:12, and complete the statement below:

They don't even know _____ ____ _____.

> *God wants us to blush over our sin and then repent.*

Israel forgot how to blush. God wants us to blush over our sin and then repent. This kind of conviction that leads to repentance is sometimes referred to as healthy shame. In her book *Shame Lifter*, Marilyn Hontz writes, "Healthy shame ought to lead us toward repentance and restoration, healing and forgiveness."[4] Healthy shame is not to be confused with the toxic shame that comes from our enemy, Satan, who leads us to feelings of worthlessness and judgment. God never wants us to live in a place of hopelessness paralyzed with feelings of failure. While that kind of shame is the devil's game, the conviction of the Holy Spirit is intended to help us guard our hearts and protect them. God's desire is for us to lead pure lives.

God never wants us to live in a place of hopelessness paralyzed with feelings of failure.

Write Proverbs 4:23 below:

Guarding our hearts will help us keep blushing as we should. We have to be careful about what we allow to influence our hearts.

Consider what influences your heart. Write one or two short statements about how the following things can affect your heart—both positively and negatively:

TV shows and movies:

Music:

Books and magazines:

People you talk to regularly:

Circumstances:

What are some practical ways we can guard our hearts from negative influences?

> *One of the best ways to guard our hearts is to guard our minds, because heart attitudes are largely determined by our thoughts.*

What goes into, or influences, our hearts, directly affects what comes out of our hearts. As we saw at the beginning of the week, Jesus said, "What you say flows from what is in your heart" (Luke 6:45b). So by guarding our hearts, we also are guarding what comes out of our mouths. One of the best ways to guard our hearts is to guard our minds, because heart attitudes are largely determined by our thoughts. Jeremiah often warned the people about their thought lives and words:

> *O Jerusalem, cleanse your heart*
> *that you may be saved.*
> *How long will you harbor*
> *your evil thoughts?*
> Jeremiah 4:14

> *"But I will be merciful only if you stop your evil thoughts and deeds and start treating each other with justice."*
> Jeremiah 7:5

Now look up Jeremiah 9:3-9 and write the ways that Judah's sin evidenced itself from their evil hearts:

Guarding our hearts means using caution about what we allow to influence our thoughts, words, and actions. It doesn't mean we close ourselves off from difficult people or painful circumstances. It also doesn't mean we totally isolate ourselves from our culture. We must figure out how to live in this world without allowing our hearts to become attached to it.

Take a few minutes to consider your thought life. Reflect on the following questions:

- Do you ever allow yourself to daydream about things you shouldn't?
- Do you tend to dwell on others' faults?
- Do you sometimes replay scenarios over and over, allowing bitterness, envy, or worry to creep in?
- Do you regularly focus your mind on trusting and believing God?

Write a prayer below, confessing any areas that need to change.

Read 2 Corinthians 10:5 in the margin. What does this verse tell us to do?

> *We destroy every proud obstacle that keeps people from knowing God. We capture their rebellious thoughts and teach them to obey Christ.*
>
> **2 Corinthians 10:5**

What thought patterns need to be "locked up" in your life?

Read Through Jeremiah:

Read Jeremiah 31–32.

Now consider your words. Ephesians 4:29 reminds us, "Don't use foul or abusive language. Let everything you say be good and helpful, so that your words will be an encouragement to those who hear them." Have you lost your shock factor—not just in foul language but also in regard to gossip, disrespect, reckless speech, or angry words? Are the majority of your words helpful to those who hear them?

Identify at least one way your talking habits need to change:

> *God longs for us to keep our hearts soft so that we are grieved when inappropriate behaviors are considered acceptable. He asks us to guard what we allow to flow both in and out of our hearts.*

In a world that offers easy and instant access to an overwhelming amount of information and stimuli, guarding our hearts takes great intentionality. With remotes, keyboards, and touch screens increasing our exposure to harmful influences, we can easily become desensitized. God longs for us to keep our hearts soft so that we are grieved when inappropriate behaviors are considered acceptable. He asks us to guard what we allow to flow both in and out of our hearts. Allowing the Holy Spirit and God's Word to be our "filter" helps keep our words and actions from damaging our hearts as well as the hearts of those around us.

Talk with God

Ask God to teach you how to guard your heart. Tell Him you want to remember how to blush and how to keep your shock factor. Pour out your heart to Him.

Day 5: With All Your Heart

In my 6:00 a.m. aerobics class, I regularly hear John Mayer's song *Half of My Heart*. In the song he laments that he finds it hard to love with only half of his heart, yet this is all he can seem to give. He basically says that he is too selfish to give his girlfriend his whole heart, admitting he's a man who has "never truly loved anything."

I've thought a lot about the lyrics, which are reminiscent of a mega theme in God's Word. Over and over God talks about those who had a whole heart for God (for example, David, Caleb, Joseph) and those who were halfhearted in their pursuit of Him (for example, Saul, Solomon, Amaziah).

Let's look at the short chapter of Jeremiah 24 to see what God says about halfheartedness.

Read Jeremiah 24 and answer these questions:

What type of fruit did God show Jeremiah in this vision?

What did the good fruit represent?

What did the rotten fruit represent?

What does verse 7 say about the hearts of the good figs?

God doesn't want half of our hearts. In the American church, we have become too much like the Israelites in Jeremiah's day. They gave God their leftovers. The figs talked about in this passage were located at the front of the Temple. This is where people brought their offerings to the Lord. They were supposed to give God their firstfruits, the best of what they harvested. When people lost faith in God's power, and perhaps even His very existence, they kept the best for themselves and put their rotten leftovers in the offering baskets at the Temple.

Similarly, our offerings to God reveal what we really believe about Him. We may attend church sporadically, say prayers at dinner, and do just enough to assuage our conscience and help us feel "spiritual enough"; but often we put more time and intentionality into planning our next vacation or our children's birthday parties and keeping up with our work and school schedules than we do intensely pursuing God with our whole hearts. We neglect God's Word and prayer, and we can't remember the last time we shared our faith. I include myself in this "we." While offering God our leftovers, we wonder why we often seem to be losing the spiritual battle against sin and the enemy in our lives. We need to pursue God wholeheartedly. We need to remember Ephesians 5:15-17: "So be careful how you live. Don't live like fools, but like those who are wise. Make the most of every opportunity in these evil days. Don't act thoughtlessly, but understand what the Lord wants you to do."

> *Often we put more time and intentionality into planning our next vacation or our children's birthday parties . . . than we do intensely pursuing God with our whole hearts.*

Read Jeremiah 29:13 in the margin. What does this verse tell us?

God wants us to live a sold-out, on fire, radical, wholehearted life in deep relationship with Him.

King Zedekiah was a halfhearted king. If you look throughout Jeremiah's prophecy, you'll find a great contrast between Zedekiah's life and Jeremiah's life. Below is a chart showing some evidences of what flowed out of each man's heart.

Circle the contrasting word or words in each line to highlight how their lives were different. The first one is done for you.

Zedekiah	Jeremiah
(Didn't listen) to what the Lord said through Jeremiah. (37:2)	(Listened) to God and proclaimed His messages. (7:1-3; 18:1-12)
Tried to solve the nation's problems through political alliances with Egypt. (37:5)	Consistently preached that the only victory would come through surrender. (38:18)
Cared more about what others thought of him than following God. He rescued Jeremiah from jail secretly; but when others pressured him to have Jeremiah put in a deep cistern, he was easily persuaded. (38:5)	Cared more about what God wanted him to do than about what others thought. (17:11-18)
Allowed fear of surrender to matter more than obeying God. (38:19)	Obeyed God wholeheartedly even though it usually brought him difficult circumstances (jail, starvation, whipping, mud-filled cistern, captivity in Egypt) (Chapter 38)
Was a coward; tried to slip away when the enemy invaded but ended up having to watch his children being murdered; then his eyes were gouged out and he was marched to Babylon. (39:4-7)	Was bold; although he wasn't perfect, he spent his life following God no matter what the cost to him personally. After Zedekiah was killed, the captain of the Babylonian guard found Jeremiah, took off his chains, and gave him freedom, food, and money. (40:4-5)

Looking at the contrast on paper, it's easy to want to have a whole heart for God. However, when difficulty and struggle come, clinging to what we cannot see and having faith to obey God's counterculture message is tougher than it sounds. It's easier to trust in tangible things such as people, money, and human effort.

Look up these verses and write a sentence summarizing each:

2 Chronicles 16:9

Psalm 103:1

Half of our hearts won't do. God created us for fullness of life; and although sin has marred God's original design, He redeems us through Christ. God doesn't desire all of our hearts because He is possessive or controlling; He simply knows that we are designed for intimacy with Him. He knows that our halfhearted attempts at following Him will lead only to dissatisfaction, complacency, and mediocrity—leaving us wanting something more. When we don't find our satisfaction in God, we tend to look to empty substitutes that can never satisfy. So God calls us to wholehearted devotion, and He leads us by His own example—not sparing His only Son to show us His wholehearted affection.

God doesn't desire all of our hearts because He is possessive or controlling; He simply knows that we are designed for intimacy with Him.

What are some areas in your spiritual life that reveal halfhearted devotion?

What practical steps can you take in order to pursue God whole-heartedly?

> *God offers us hope and healing as we surrender our broken hearts to Him. God calls us to trust Him and to dare to hope in Him— even with the most fragile of hearts.*

This week we've been talking about keeping a soft heart devoted wholly to God. Dealing with our heart issues isn't always easy. Many of us have been hurt deeply by others, whether through abuse, neglect, or rejection. Others of us may not have suffered as much, but we still need to work through the daily wear and tear on our hearts as we live in a fallen world. God offers us hope and healing as we surrender our broken hearts to Him. God calls us to trust Him and to dare to hope in Him—even with the most fragile of hearts.

As we close, take a minute to review the five themes from the week. You might call them "heart cautions."

Circle the heart caution that speaks most loudly to you personally:

1. Be careful to evaluate your own heart.

2. Be careful not to confuse behavior modification with heart change.

3. Be careful to bring your hurting heart to God.

4. Be careful to guard your heart.

5. Be careful to seek God wholeheartedly.

Talk with God

Ask God to continue His work in your heart. Take some time being still before Him now. Look at the heart caution you circled on the previous page. Turn back to that day's lesson and skim through it while asking God to reveal one truth He wants you to meditate on. Write that truth below, and then spend some time in God's presence, letting Him speak His whole-hearted love over you, His precious daughter.

Read Through Jeremiah:

Read Jeremiah 33–34.

Digging Deeper

How did Jeremiah deal with his loneliness as he pursued a close relationship with God? To learn about Jeremiah's relationship with Baruch and why we all need godly friends as we travel the road of life, go to AbingdonWomen.com/Jeremiah and read Digging Deeper Week 4: "Somewhere Along the Road."

Video Viewer Guide

WEEK 4:
STAYING SPIRITUALLY SENSITIVE

Heart Issues

Guard your heart above all else,

   for it determines the course of your life.

Proverbs 4:23 NLT

Heavy Heart Clothes

1. Greed

"From the least to the greatest,

   their lives are _____ by _____."

Jeremiah 6:13 NLT

2. Deceit

When we tell lies about _____, it can cause us to tell lies about

_____.

3. Stubbornness

I'm not going to be _____;

I'm not going to be _____;

I'm not willing to _____.

4. Hardness

"The sin of Judah

   is inscribed with an iron chisel—

engraved with a diamond point on their _____ hearts

   and on the corners of their altars."

Jeremiah 17:1 NLT

5. Antagonism

When we are looking for a _____.

VIDEO VIEWER GUIDE: WEEK 4

6. Pride

O people of Judah and Jerusalem,

> *surrender your _____ and _____.*

Change your hearts before the Lord …

   Jeremiah 4:4 NLT

Our culture tells us to follow our heart. God's Word tells us:

"The human heart is the most deceitful of all things,

> *and desperately wicked.*
> *Who really knows how bad it is?"*

   Jeremiah 17:9 NLT

Take time to do a _____ _____.

We have to bring our hearts to God so that He can _____ them.

_____ modification ≠ heart change.

Your name is on their _____,

> *but you are far from their _____.*

   Jeremiah 12:2b NLT

When we bring our hearts to God, He takes off our heavy heart clothes and gives us a new, lighter spiritual wardrobe:

greed ⟶ generosity   hardness ⟶ softness

deceit ⟶ truth   antagonism ⟶ peace

stubbornness ⟶ flexibility   pride ⟶ humility

Week 5

QUITTING THE
BLAME GAME
Personal Responsibility

Memory Verse

This is what the LORD says:
"Don't let the wise boast in their wisdom,
*   or the powerful boast in their power,*
*   or the rich boast in their riches.*
But those who wish to boast
*   should boast in this alone:*
that they truly know me and understand that I am the LORD. . . ."
                                    Jeremiah 9:23-24

Fun Fact:

Jeremiah is the twenty-fourth book in the Bible.

Day 1: Good Discipline

I love summer when my delightful children are home from school. The good news is that it gives me a great opportunity for training as they work out conflicts with one another. The bad news is that this exhausts me to no end. The thing that gets under my skin the most as a parent is all the blaming. One sibling says that another sibling is to blame for his or her failure to complete a chore or make a wise choice. Then when I investigate and point out the blaming child's own sin or failure in the situation, the blame can quickly turn to me. I'm told that I make unfair decisions, expect too much, or don't understand their preteen lives. My discipline or consequences are viewed as measures to "ruin their lives." Over and over I try to explain that if I didn't care, I wouldn't take the time and energy to correct, train, pray, and discipline.

Proverbs says that parents who don't love their children fail to discipline them (13:24). In the Book of Jeremiah, the many passages that include God's judgment can fly in the face of our theology of God's love and mercy. However, today we will explore how God's justice and mercy hold hands as He disciplines His children like a good father.

> *Those who spare the rod of discipline hate their children.*
> *Those who love their children care enough to discipline them.*
>
> **Proverbs 13:24**

Jeremiah's prophet status did not exempt him from making complaints and asking honest questions. He knew just where to take them.

Read Jeremiah 12:1-4. Write the two questions Jeremiah brought to his Maker in the first verse:

1.

2.

In verse 2 we learn these wicked but happy people are not those of the surrounding pagan nations. Instead, these people have God's name on their lips though their hearts are a million miles away. Jeremiah sacrificed everything in his pursuit of God. He lost the approval of his family, his safety, and his status in society; God even instructed him not to marry and have children. Yet those around him who were speaking God's name but not living the life to back up their words seemed to be happy, healthy, and living the good life.

Have you ever compared yourself with others around you and thought God was unjust? Write below a current or past frustration with what seems or seemed like an unfair situation in your life:

Now hold that thought, and we'll come back to it in a minute.

Read Jeremiah 12:5-13 to find the Lord's reply to Jeremiah's complaint. God answered with two questions for Jeremiah.

What physical illustrations did God use in these questions?

What was the message God was repeating?

God allows our questions, but He also helps us get some much-needed perspective on our situation. God was cautioning Jeremiah through these two physical illustrations, reminding him where he should put his hope and confidence. We can sum it up in three words: *trust me alone.*

I have been learning this the hard way lately. God has been saying to me through these verses in Jeremiah, "If you think this situation is hard, dig up your tree and plant it a little closer to the riverbank. Your own brothers and sisters will turn against you with plots and complaints; don't trust anyone but Me."

Of course, God wants us to live in community and to have friends and family. He isn't calling us to put up huge walls around our hearts and shut everyone out. The issue here is our ultimate "safe place." If we elevate anything or anyone above God in our lives, we will find our perspective of justice becomes warped. When we look to people or circumstances to find our identity, they will ultimately fail to fill our God-shaped hole. When we feel this emptiness, we must be careful to trust God instead of trying to figure out what is "fair" and "unfair" according to our limited view.

In the unfair situation you named earlier, consider how the message of *trust me alone* needs to be applied (or could have been applied). Write some notes below:

Through Jeremiah 12:5-13, God responds to our questions about justice, saying essentially: "If you think this is tough or unfair, brace yourself. Transfer your trust from any person or thing to My care, or the ride ahead may be rocky." He is not threatening us in any way but warning us to continually trust in His sovereignty because He knows the dangers of reverting to our human strength. This message echoes the theme of idolatry from Week 2. When we believe our security is found in relationships, status, possessions, or anything else, God is willing to allow the ground beneath our feet to shake in order to see if we remember where our true foundation lies. As the old hymn "My Hope Is Built" reminds us, "On Christ the solid rock I stand, *all* other ground is sinking sand"[1] (emphasis added).

> *God allows our questions, but He also helps us get some much-needed perspective on our situation.*

> *When we believe our security is found in relationships, status, possessions, or anything else, God is willing to allow the ground beneath our feet to shake in order to see if we remember where our true foundation lies.*

God essentially asks Jeremiah, "If you are perplexed when phony people appear to be happy, then what will you do when your own brothers turn against you?" Ouch. I've experienced some testing of my own places where I turn to find security. Though I claim God as my safe place, ugly idols can creep in, trying to usurp the number-one place in my life. I couldn't believe how quickly healthy relationships had become harmful because I had held them too tightly. This is where devoted God-followers are separated from those who are just giving God lip service. If racing against people makes us tired, how will we fare in the horse race if we attempt to run in our own strength?

With the trust issue settled, God goes on to explain Himself briefly to Jeremiah, giving him a little sneak peek into the journey ahead. I am grateful God doesn't always give me this kind of glimpse. I'm glad He didn't spell out to me in high school all the details of what lay ahead for me. So much of it has been thrilling, but the details of childbirth, sickness, heartbreak, and cross-country moves were better left to tackle as they came. Sometimes it's easier to take life one day at a time. No need for sneak peeks. Yet as God's prophet to Judah, Jeremiah has the coming destruction spelled out for him.

Read Jeremiah 12:7-13. What are a few of the word pictures God employs to paint a picture of the future in these verses?

In verse 13, God speaks of a harvest. What does He say the crop will be?

> *When we plant seeds of rebellion, closed ears, and idolatry, we reap a harvest of shame and consequences.*

Here we see a principle found throughout God's Word: sowing and reaping. Galatians 6:7 says that "God is not mocked, for you reap whatever you sow" (NRSV). When we plant seeds of rebellion, closed ears, and idolatry, we reap a harvest of shame and consequences. The people of Judah found this out the hard way: they lived it.

What lessons have you had to learn the hard way according to the sowing and reaping principle?

We need this reminder about sowing and reaping so that when we read the passages in Jeremiah about the harsh realities of war, exile, and poverty that God allowed, we don't become like the Israelites living in Judah who viewed God as unfair, unwilling, and unloving. These aren't passages we should be embarrassed about or want to hide in favor of New Testament verses about love and grace. God's message is consistent.

Let's look at some verses in Jeremiah to understand why God allows such great difficulty in the lives of His people.

Write what you learn about God's justice and/or mercy in the following passages:

Verse	Justice	Mercy
2:14-17		
7:3		
30:11-15		
31:20		
36:6-7		
46:28		

Fun Fact:

Jeremiah served under the following kings:
Josiah
Jehoahaz
Jehoiakim
Jehoiachin
Zedekiah

In one or two sentences, how would you sum up these verses about why God allowed the people to be defeated by Babylon and to face hardships?

Now, let's bring it a little closer to home. Why does God allow difficulty or suffering in our lives—in *your* life? I wish we could answer this in a paragraph with a neat, easy answer. But there are no easy answers when it comes to suffering.

Let's examine three categories of suffering:

1. First, we suffer because we live in a fallen, sinful world. After Eve and Adam ate the forbidden fruit, sin entered the world. As a result, disease, violence, and the wrong choices made by others affect us just because we live on this planet. Romans 8:20a says, "Against its will, all creation was subjected to God's curse." Much of our suffering is the result of being born into a world marked by sin—from the weeds in our gardens to the pain of childbirth and the many other effects of the rebellion back in Genesis.

2. Other times we suffer because of our obedience to God. Jeremiah followed God wholeheartedly and yet he was beaten, put in chains, jailed, and lowered into a mud-filled cistern to die. These trials were not consequences of bad decisions. They were the result of living in a sinful world that is hostile to the things of God. Yet instead of moping and blaming God (okay, Jeremiah did do a little moping; see 20:14-18), Jeremiah trusted God. Even if his rescue wouldn't come until the next life, he put his trust in the Lord of Heaven's Armies, and God sustained Jeremiah through the difficulties. Paul also said this would be true for us as well in 2 Timothy 3:12, "Yes, and everyone who wants to live a godly life in Christ Jesus will suffer persecution." Our persecution may not include physical hardship, but following God's way will include some pushback from others at times.

3. However, suffering can also be the result of bad choices that we make. When we overspend habitually, we can't be mad at God because we can't pay our bills. When we choose to treat our bodies, God's temple, with neglect from habitual unhealthy eating,

poor sleeping habits, and lack of exercise, we can't blame God for the related health problems. When we live on a spiritual diet of TV, magazines, media, gossip, and other soul junk food, we can't blame God that we don't experience victory over sin. When we neglect to take the time to prayerfully discipline our children, there are sure to be consequences.

God is a good daddy. He uses whatever is necessary to get His children's attention when we are making terrible decisions. God is willing to watch us suffer if that's what it takes to bring us back into relationship with Him. Just as we must allow discomfort in our children's lives when they rebel, disobey, and make unwise choices, God is the perfect parent in our lives, allowing us to reap what we sow in order to draw us back to Him.

> *God is the perfect parent in our lives, allowing us to reap what we sow in order to draw us back to Him.*

Jeremiah is not the only book in the Bible where we see God's discipline. In Deuteronomy 8, Moses reminds the people of their consequences in the wilderness. Then he says, "Think about it: Just as a parent disciplines a child, the LORD your God disciplines you for your own good" (v. 5). Because God is just, He allows consequences. However, He always does this out of His great love for us. In fact, He was willing to make the ultimate sacrifice on our behalf, sending His own Son to die in our place in order to deal with our sin.

When we are tempted to blame God for hard or painful things in life, we need to remember His character and trust His goodness—especially when we don't understand our circumstances.

Read Hebrews 12:5-12. How do these verses in Hebrews relate to the verses in Jeremiah about the Lord's discipline (see the chart on page 139)?

If you are God's child, He is probably faithfully disciplining you in at least one area right now. Where do you see Him allowing consequences in your life (relationships, finances, marital issues, parenting, time management, ministry, and so on)?

Read Through Jeremiah:

Read Jeremiah 35–36.

How does today's lesson change your perspective about God's heart in what He is trying to accomplish in your life?

Talk with God

Spend some time in prayer, asking God for comfort from whatever suffering you are enduring right now. Ask God to give you wisdom to know whether the cause of your pain is from living in a fallen world, persecution for following Jesus, or possibly discipline related to some issue in your life. Look for His Father's heart behind whatever correction He is giving and seek to be a teachable child.

Day 2: Finding a Target

When I was a kid, my dad occasionally would wake everyone in the house and call us to hunt for his lost keys so that he could leave for work. The apple doesn't fall far from the tree, only with me it's my cell phone. I never remember where I left it and often blame my kids or husband for moving it. Usually I find it in my purse or jacket pocket—right where I left it. Until it is found, I am sure that someone else is to blame. It's humbling when the facts prove that my accusations are unfounded.

> *This is what the LORD says: "Cursed are those who put their trust in mere humans, who rely on human strength and turn their hearts away from the LORD."*
>
> **Jeremiah 17:5**

The people of Judah had problems with blaming as well. They often claimed they were innocent of wrongdoing and denied that they worshiped idols (Jeremiah 2:23). They did not want to take personal responsibility for playing a part in the consequences headed their way. God didn't leave them to wonder why they were headed for judgment. In Jeremiah 17:5 we find God clearly communicating His answer to the question *Why?* The judgments of God against the people of Judah—which consisted of war, poverty, hunger, exile, and utter defeat—were the result of their own sin. God wasn't shy about being specific about His people's offenses.

Look up the following verses in Jeremiah, and draw a line from the reference on the left to God's description of the people's behavior on the right.

5:6   you have not changed
                                        your ways

5:7   you have forsaken the
                                        covenant of your God and
                                        worshiped other gods

15:6   you have followed your own
                                        desires and have not obeyed me

6:17   your rebellion is great

6:19   your children have forsaken me;
                                        you committed adultery

16:12   you would not listen to
                                        my watchmen

15:7   you have abandoned/
                                        rejected me

22:8-9   you refused to listen/
                                        rejected my word/law

As you review the right column above, what correlations or similarities to our culture do you see?

Do you see anything in the list that strikes a chord of conviction in your own life?

God did not leave the people of Judah to wonder why these terrible circumstances were upon them. He was clear. If they wanted to blame someone, they needed to hold up a mirror. They shouldn't have been surprised at God's heavy hand against them. He laid out instructions for them when they first entered the land seven hundred years earlier.

Let's turn back the pages of Scripture to see what directions God had given them. He wasn't a parent who expected His children to read His mind about His expectations. He gave them clear instructions, spelling out both the consequences of disobedience and the blessings of obedience.

Read Deuteronomy 30:11-20 and answer the following questions:

Was God's message or command difficult to understand or beyond their reach? (vv. 11-14)

What was the choice that was laid out before the people? (v. 15)

What did they need to do, and what would be the result of this choice? (v. 16)

What were they warned not to do, and what was the consequence for doing this? (vv. 17-18)

What did God want them to choose? (v. 19)

Now read Jeremiah 21:8-9 in the margin. How do these verses echo back to the Deuteronomy passage?

God put two choices before His people—life or death. He instructed His people, and when they got off course, He sent His prophets to repeat the message. Since sin entered the world, God's message has been the same: "Turn from your sins and turn to me." Both John the Baptist (Luke 3:3) and Jesus (Matthew 4:17) came preaching this message.

It's easy to look at the people of Judah and think they were crazy not to follow and love God. After all, they had been given clear instructions, they had the warnings of the prophets calling them to repent, and they even had the example of their neighbors in Israel, who were reaping the consequences of their own sin. (Israel, the Northern Kingdom, had gone into captivity one hundred years before Babylon invaded Judah.) Yet in Jeremiah 3:6-10, we see God telling the people of Judah that they didn't learn from the sins of Israel. Though they had the law and the prophets, they chose not to heed the warnings and to stubbornly "eat the bitter fruit of living their own way" (Proverbs 1:31).

Are we so different? Who do you blame when life gets rough? Human nature calls out, "It's not my fault! If only I had a great marriage . . . If only my kids behaved like so and so's kids . . . If only I had more money . . . If only my friends supported me . . . If only I was appreciated at work . . ." No matter where we choose to place the blame, the truth is that we need to get honest about our own failures. Are we loving God, walking in His ways and following His commands as laid out in Deuteronomy? Do our prayer lives reflect it? Do our financial choices show that God is our priority? Do we regularly serve others and share our faith? Does our heart break for the things that break God's heart? Could it be that the problem lies within us?

Let's take inventory of what we have today:

- Clear instructions on how to live from the complete Word of God.
- Access to great preaching, teaching, and Bible studies through our local churches and Christian media.

- Examples of many who have chosen not to walk with God and are eating the bitter fruit of their choices.
- Examples of many others who are living radically for Christ.

We can't change anyone else, but we can allow God to change us.

If anything, I believe we could be held more accountable than the people of Jeremiah's day because of the opportunity we have to know and study the truth. We have God's Word in its entirety, as well as the indwelling Holy Spirit to guide us in applying it. It's time to stop blaming others for our problems, take a good look at our own sin, and begin to walk the road of repentance. We can't change anyone else, but we can allow God to change us.

1. Take a moment to list the difficult things in your life right now in the following categories:

    Relationships (friends, marriage, children, coworkers)

    Financial Issues

    Time Commitments

    Personal Health

    Emotional Issues

    Spiritual Issues

2. Now draw a star beside those things that are completely beyond your control (nothing you do or don't do will affect the outcome).

3. Everything else on the list could be a consequence of bad choices. Circle any that you think might be.

Read Through Jeremiah:

Read Jeremiah 37–38.

Today we delved into one of my least favorite topics—the tendency we all have toward passing the buck. As frustrated as I can get with my children's overt attempts to explain away their bad choices, I know I'm also often looking for a target to blame. Just as I desire my kids to own up to their mistakes so that they can learn from them, God wants us turn from our sin so that we can turn to Him. He wants to give us mercy, and He calls us to recognize our bad choices and repent. I'm thankful that as we evaluate our lives and seek to take whatever steps necessary to follow Him, He redeems even our mistakes to bring us into closer relationship with Him.

> *If we claim we have no sin, we are only fooling ourselves and not living in the truth.*
>
> *But if we confess our sins to him, he is faithful and just to forgive us our sins and to cleanse us from all wickedness.*
>
> **1 John 1:8-9**

Talk with God

Submit yourself to God's discipline in the areas you circled. Ask Him to show you where you haven't fully surrendered to Him. Repent of any sin and confess that you want to walk in obedience to Christ. Take some time to wait and listen in His presence. In the margin, write anything God tells you in regard to sin patterns or habits that are bringing consequences in your life.

Day 3: Perilous Pride

When I was pregnant with our twins, I became really sick. Even though I thought I was only having one baby until ten days before they were born, the reality of double girl hormones wasn't lost on my body. I couldn't keep much food down for around twenty weeks. I can't call it morning sickness because it was more like all-day sickness. My son was three-and-a-half at the time and very active. I am not the gal who likes to admit I can't do something, especially something like taking care of one child.

My favorite movie line is from *The Rookie*; the main character says he should stop pursuing his dream of playing baseball to come home and help his wife, and she replies, "I'm a Texas woman, which means I don't need the help of a man to keep things running."[3] I want to be like her—independent and able to take care of everything without needing the help of others.

It pained me to admit I could do little more than lie in bed, moan, and try to keep down what food I could manage. I remember a friend from church I barely knew stopping by to pick up my son for the afternoon so I could rest. She always teases me now about my disheveled hair, bathrobe, and murmuring some instructions about how to take care of him. Those days were humbling. I hated the feeling of being dependent on others and did a lot of moping and blaming during those dark days. While I wish I could say I drew close to the Lord during that time, in reality I did a lot of wallowing in self-pity.

> *We all battle daily against the sin of pride, and we will fight it until the day we are free from sin forever in heaven with Jesus.*

The words *pride* and *proud* are mentioned in the Book of Jeremiah numerous times, warranting a day of focus in our study. Pride is an elusive thing. It can take many forms. Simply put, it is an obsession with self. Apart from God's work in our lives, every one of us will make decisions to serve our own interests—to paint ourselves in the best light and work out situations to our benefit. This is the core of our sin problem. We all battle daily against the sin of pride, and we will fight it until the day we are free from sin forever in heaven with Jesus.

Sometimes we experience a different kind of pride called "reverse pride." This is when we are so down on ourselves that others may think it's humility. We might claim we are "no good" or "not of any value." But this is self-abasement, not humility. God says that we are fearfully and wonderfully made (see Psalm 139:14 and Jeremiah 1) and that we have great value as His children. When we put ourselves down with negative statements, such as

"I could never be good at that";
"They won't want me to come because I never add anything to the conversation";
"My nose is too big. I'm so fat. I wish I looked like her";
"I don't think I should attempt that; I probably won't be any good at it";

this is not humility. This is still pride, which demonstrates a lack of belief in what God says about our value.

The nations surrounding Israel and Judah struggled with pride. In Jeremiah 46–51, God lays out His judgments against these foreign nations. Here we see that although God has a special love for Judah, He cares about all people and gives them a chance to turn to Him. God has always loved and adopted those who wish to follow Him. We see that God is holy and holds every nation accountable for its own sins using the same standard. He calls these nations back to Himself in the same way that He indicted Judah in the previous chapters. Let's look at a few verses where God speaks to their pride issue.

Fill in the following chart to get a clearer picture of national pride and its consequences.

Jeremiah passage	Nation	Details about pride	Consequences God gives
46:8-12, 24			
48:7-9, 14-15, 29-31, 42			
49:1, 4-5, 16			
50:31-34			

How does the pride of the nations in the chart on the previous page resonate with American culture?

> "Yes, I am the vine; you are the branches. Those who remain in me, and I in them, will produce much fruit. For apart from me you can do nothing."
>
> **John 15:5**

Did you notice how these nations trusted in their "wealth and skill"? They deceived themselves into thinking that every good thing in their lives was their own doing. This resembles the American mind-sets of "I deserve it," "I am powerful," and "Look at all I have accomplished." Hard work, goal setting, and material goods are not inherently wrong, but we would be wise to always remember that "apart from [Him we] can do nothing" (John 15:5). Anything good we accomplish originated in God, who gave us the talent and resources. We need to remember the Moabites so that we will not become like them—trusting in wealth and skill while forgetting the God in heaven who has given these gifts.

Now let's turn to God's special people of Judah. Let's see if they humbled themselves in contrast to their surrounding neighbors or joined with them in perilous pride.

In the passages below, underline words or phrases that smack of pride in the lives of the people of Judah:

"They have lied about the LORD
  and said, 'He won't bother us!
No disasters will come upon us.
  There will be no war or famine.
God's prophets are all windbags
  who don't really speak for him.
    Let their predictions of disaster fall on themselves!'"

Jeremiah 5:12-13

"I will personally fight against the people in Jerusalem,
  that mighty fortress—
the people who boast, 'No one can touch us here.
  No one can break in here.'"

Jeremiah 21:13

Now look back at what you underlined and describe some evidences of Judah's pride:

How do the media portray Christianity? Give some specific examples from TV, movies, radio, magazines, or the Internet.

Do you think that the media's posture toward faith in Christ ever resembles that of the people of Judah toward Jeremiah's message? If so, in what ways?

God takes pride very seriously because it is a huge barrier to close relationship with Him. We can't embrace God until we recognize our need for Him. No clearer does He spell it out than here in Jeremiah.

> *God takes pride very seriously because it is a huge barrier to close relationship with Him.*

Read Jeremiah 9:23-24. What are we not to boast in?

What is the only thing we should boast about?

Again in Jeremiah 13:15-17, God gives a stern warning against pride. What does our pride cause Him to do?

God weeps when we become self-absorbed because we are missing out on the life He designed us to live in fellowship with Him. He knows pride will lead us to emptiness, and it breaks His heart to the point of tears.

As we've seen, our sin nature has a natural bent toward pride. None of us escapes this tendency without frequent self-evaluation and repentance. Doing regular heart and motive checks as we talked about in Week 4 can help us see when we are wearing pride without realizing it. Even the most loyal followers of God can allow pride to creep into their hearts and minds.

Another way to keep our pride in check is to have a good friend who will point it out from time to time. Jeremiah's scribe and possibly his only friend was named Baruch. (Don't forget how unpopular Jeremiah's messages made him.) Baruch recorded the messages from the Lord and sometimes delivered them to kings for Jeremiah. In Jeremiah 45, the Lord lovingly warns Baruch through Jeremiah about the danger of going down the road of self-focus.

The prophet Jeremiah gave a message to Baruch son of Neriah in the fourth year of the reign of Jehoiakim son of Josiah, after Baruch had written down everything Jeremiah had dictated to him. He said,

"This is what the Lord, the God of Israel, says to you, Baruch:

You have said, 'I am overwhelmed with trouble! Haven't I had enough pain already? And now the Lord has added more! I am worn out from sighing and can find no rest.'

"Baruch, this is what the Lord says: 'I will destroy this nation that I built. I will uproot what I planted.

Are you seeking great things for yourself? Don't do it! I will bring great disaster upon all these people; but I will give you your life as a reward wherever you go. I, the Lord, have spoken!'"

Jeremiah 45:1-5

Read Jeremiah 45:1-5 in the margin and find Baruch's complaints:

Baruch's frustrations were well-founded. He had truly suffered, just as Jeremiah had. They lived in a time when bread was scarce, enemies invaded regularly, and they publicly wrote and recorded messages that weren't popular. Though we often stroke and coddle our girlfriends when they are making a case for injustice in their lives, Jeremiah was kind but bold in his response to Baruch.

What is the warning from God that Jeremiah gives to Baruch? (v. 5)

I believe this is God's warning to us as well. Write your name in the blank below:

"Are you seeking great things for yourself,

_____?"

Now write the statement that answers this question in ALL CAPS:

Read Through Jeremiah:

Read Jeremiah 39–40.

The battle against selfish pride is clear in this passage. When we begin to walk the road of self-absorption, God says to us, "DON'T DO IT!"

When I become focused on myself, I notice a few things I would rather not admit:

- I tend to brag or name-drop about things God has done through me as if I deserved some of the credit.
- I fall into old sin patterns with my thought life, namely judging others.
- I find myself in conflicts—with my husband, my children, or my friends.
- I begin to see others for what they have or haven't done to support me.
- I worry about money and try to figure out how to solve issues on my own.

Did you notice some common words in these admissions? Me. My. Myself. Yuck. I want to pretend that it's not true and that I'm naturally humble and kind, but the reality is that apart from Jesus, my defaults smack of perilous pride.

Okay, your turn. What are some of your tendencies when pride creeps in?

I hope you thought of at least one, because my list took me all of thirty seconds to write, and I could go on! The takeaway for us today is that pride is dangerous. If we don't deal with it, we must brace ourselves for a fall. This is true for us not only on a corporate level as a nation but also on a personal level as individuals. Recognizing our pride and addressing it with God through prayer is critical if we are to stop playing the blame game.

Talk with God

Spend a few minutes confessing your pride and boasting in God. Write below three of His qualities that you can boast in today:

1.

2.

3.

Now take some time to pray for our nation. Pray specifically for humility and for our hearts to turn back to our Maker. Meditate on 2 Chronicles 7:14: "Then if my people who are called by my name will humble themselves and pray and seek my face and turn from their wicked ways, I will hear from heaven and will forgive their sins and restore their land."

Day 4: Going Through the Motions

We see in Scripture that God uses physical objects and actions to help His people understand and remember important events and spiritual truths. In the Old Testament, the Passover celebration and the sacrificial system are examples of rituals that picture God's character through physical acts. In the New Testament, baptism and Holy Communion are important physical expressions of spiritual realities.

Religious rituals become empty when our motivation is anything other than our devoted love for God.

Though religious rituals can have great significance and can be holy acts through which we experience the presence and grace of God, we must be careful not to allow them to make us feel that we are somehow "appeasing" God or fulfilling some kind of duty or obligation. Religious rituals become empty when our motivation is anything other than our devoted love for God. It's like when a husband and wife start going through the motions rather than demonstrating genuine love for each other. Who wants a spouse whose mind is always somewhere else and whose actions are perfunctory? Who wants to be given a kiss out of duty or obligation?

That's exactly what had happened to the people of Judah's worship: they were going through the motions. The priests were offering sacrifices, and false prophets were delivering messages they said were from the Lord, but their hearts were not right (see Jeremiah 23:11). Not only were they going through the motions, but they also allowed their religious practices to be corrupted by pagan influences.

Draw a line to match each passage with the correct outward expression:

7:8-11, 30-34   detestable things/evils/
                                 abominations

9:25-26   attendance/worship in the Temple

11:15-17   circumcision

How would you summarize what God thought of their religious practices?

Fun Fact:

Limestone caves in Palestine were used as robbers' dens. They were temporary hideouts between crimes. This is Jeremiah's allusion to the Temple in 7:11.

The people felt justified or "right with God" because they had the Temple, which they believed always would be protected by God. As one source explains, "Many Jews thought that if they were in the house of God then they would be under God's protection, and as a result [they] tended to be careless in their daily living."[4] They also expanded their religious practices as a sort of backup plan. Just in case God wasn't strong enough to save them, they would sacrifice their sons and daughters to pagan gods who might be able to help them. They went to great lengths and expense to try to persuade any god who might listen to help them. Even though they had little money, they would waste drink offerings to pour out to a foreign god referred to as the Queen of Heaven or buy little handmade statues in the town square that were carved in the images of other gods. But all of these practices were empty.

As we read in Jeremiah 9:25-26, God was not pleased with their empty practice of circumcision. Circumcision, which was instituted by God during the days of Abraham to set the Israelites apart, was a symbol meant to remind the people of their covenant with God (Genesis 17:9-14). The people kept the practice but forgot the spiritual significance behind the ritual. Even here in the Old Testament God is talking about a circumcision of the heart.

Read Romans 2:29 in the margin. What does it tell us about circumcision of the heart?

> *No, a true Jew is one whose heart is right with God. And true circumcision is not merely obeying the letter of the law; rather, it is a change of heart produced by God's Spirit. And a person with a changed heart seeks praise from God, not from people.*
>
> **Romans 2:29**

In Jeremiah's day, God's original intent for the practices was lost. The people attempted to go through the motions, and then they added horrific rituals from pagan religions, which only added to their shame. What might they have said to justify this? Try to imagine the women chatting at the well, explaining themselves, calling God unfair, and spinning the details so that others would sympathize with them:

"We've done everything God said. We've given our sacrifices, circumcised our sons, visited the Temple, and tried to keep the Sabbath when nothing else was going on. Well, we've done almost everything, I guess. I mean, nobody's perfect. We have given some offerings to Baal and the Queen of Heaven, and we might have burned our children in sacrifice to these gods; but if the Lord doesn't think they're real gods, then what does it matter to Him? As long as we give Him our offerings, why should He care what we do on the side?"

Before we judge the women of Judah, we must ask ourselves if we've ever gone through the motions or made our own determinations about what God should or shouldn't care about. We cannot blame Him for our partial obedience, our halfhearted attempts at following Him, and our blatant disobedience. We do not worship a god we create according to what makes sense to our mind, will, and emotions. We worship the sovereign God of the Bible, the Creator of the universe, the Lord of Heaven's Armies. God is who He says He is in His Word. This is why we must read and study the Bible curiously and carefully, seeking to know the true God. Knowing God gives us the passion to keep our devotional time, church attendance, and ministry involvement from becoming rote, empty expressions.

Sometimes we assume that God owes us a pain-free life because we have done "our part." We went to church services twice last month and even dropped a twenty-dolllar-bill in the offering plate. We made sure our kids took the right church classes, said the right spiritual words, and jumped through all the religious hoops. Then when something bad happens, we are tempted to blame God since we have paid our dues. But it doesn't work that way.

Fun Fact:

Chapter 14 marks the third time the Lord tells Jeremiah not to pray for the people of Judah because of their lack of true repentance.

While you might nod your head, agreeing that this is wrong thinking, these thoughts can infiltrate our minds at times. I talked with a mom recently whose husband had just lost his job. At the end of the conversation she made an offhanded comment, saying that God had better come through for them because they had come through for Him all their lives. I'm sure she didn't mean God owed her something—or did she? When things go wrong in my own life, I can find the same line of thinking infecting the way I process my trials. None of us is immune to finding ourselves blaming God, especially when we are in pain.

> *None of us is immune to finding ourselves blaming God, especially when we are in pain.*

Think about your spiritual habits in the following areas. Put a check mark beside any that have become empty religious routines where you are just going through the motions. Be honest with yourself.

_____ reading God's Word

_____ prayer life

_____ church attendance/worship

_____ ministry involvement/service

_____ Bible study/small group

_____ Holy Communion

_____ other:_____

Spiritual rhythms or disciplines can be great connecting points with God in our lives. Going to church, spending time in prayer, and reading God's Word lead us into deeper relationship with Him. The danger comes when our religious practices become rote and stale. We must constantly seek to find the meaning in our routines to keep them fresh.

Talk with God

Review the list of spiritual habits above, and then ask God to show you some action steps you can take to infuse new life and spirit into any empty or lifeless areas. On the next page are some ideas to prayerfully consider. Put a check mark next to any that you feel God is calling you to act on, and then continue to pray and listen. Make a commitment to "shake it up" as God directs.

Read Through Jeremiah:

Read Jeremiah 41–42.

___ Change the time or place of your Bible reading or use a different Bible translation.

___ Make a change in where you serve.

___ Go out on a Spirit-led limb and try something big.

___ Consider leaving your small group and starting a new one. (God is into multiplication.)

___ Find an accountability partner to regularly ask how your prayer life is going.

___ Change your posture of worship (silently meditate on the words of Scripture, close your eyes while you sing, kneel or raise your hand in praise, and so on).

___ Fast for a day and review why you do what you do with your time, talent, and treasure.

___ Try journaling.

___ Begin memorizing Scripture (or memorize a large passage if you already memorize Scripture).

___ Commit to pray for another country.

___ Go on a mission trip.

Day 5: Rescue with Repentance

Two important people in my life struggle with anger. Both love God passionately and care about their families. Both have offered apologies and expressed regret repeatedly for outbursts they wish they could take back. I believe this has contributed to my lack of enthusiasm about apologies. I reached the point when I didn't want another apology. I wanted the outbursts to stop. I wanted to feel peaceful instead of anxious, anticipating when their anger might erupt again. Both of these people have come a long way in their battle with anger, but I cannot say the scar of empty words hasn't stayed with me.

Words are important. They have the power of life and death according to Proverbs 18:21. However, words of intent without follow-through are just wishful thinking. They are the New Year's resolutions we make without a plan to see them through. They are the apologies we offer even when it's obvious we don't mean it. They are the promises we make to God but don't keep, such as saying that we love God but refusing to get along with His children. They are empty words with no actions to back them up.

> *The tongue can bring death or life; those who love to talk will reap the consequences.*
>
> **Proverbs 18:21**

The people of Judah had a lot of experience in offering empty words. They cried out to God on several occasions, declaring their intent to change their ways, but there were no actions to back up their words.

Jeremiah spoke often about repentance. One source notes that "the Hebrew word most often used by Jeremiah for repentance is *sub*, usually translated 'return' or 'turn.' It is a key word in Jeremiah, who interpreted repentance as a reorientation of one's life, that is, a turning away from sin and a simultaneous turning to God."[5]

Have you ever been driving the wrong way and your smart phone or GPS said, "Recalculating"? Then it rerouted you so that you were turned back toward your destination rather than away from it. A similar concept happens in life when we get off course spiritually. Once we acknowledge we are moving in the wrong direction, we must turn around—repent—and go God's new way, which gets us to the destination of intimacy with Him.

Read Jeremiah 14:1-10.

What words or phrases seem to communicate repentance? (v. 7)

How did the people question and blame God? (vv. 8-9)

It would seem that they are crying out to God for rescue, but what does God say about their behavior? (v. 10)

The people were crying out for rescue, but God knew their hearts. Their motives weren't right. They wanted God's hand of help without any relationship or repentance. It's like the rebellious teenager who consistently makes bad choices but then wants to be bailed out of the penalties every time. Softening the pain of consequences won't help the teen to change. Like a good parent, God chose to allow Judah to experience the difficulty brought upon them by their bad decisions.

God used this same standard for other nations as well.

> *Destroying armies come against Babylon. Her mighty men are captured, and their weapons break in their hands. For the Lord is a God who gives just punishment; he always repays in full.*
>
> **Jeremiah 51:56**

Read Jeremiah 51:56 in the margin and rewrite it below in your own words.

What does this verse tell us about God's character?

This helps us understand why the cross is so significant. Sin must be punished. God is holy and cannot tolerate sin. In Week 6 we will talk about the hope that God continually offers us as seen through the Book of Jeremiah. This hope centers on Jeremiah's prediction of a future Messiah. Although Jeremiah did not know Jesus' name, His faith in the future Savior assured his salvation as much as my faith in Jesus does. Jesus' sacrifice on the cross was the necessary payment for our sin so that we can be in relationship with God. This is the good news of the gospel. However, the gospel message also includes repentance.

Repentance is not just admitting our sin; it is *turning* from it. God wants more than words. Real faith reveals itself through actions. It turns away from sin and toward a holy God. Let us learn from the people of Judah and the Babylonians that God wants us to fully yield our words and our lives to Him. When our mouths say one thing but our actions reveal something else, we are only lying to ourselves.

Let's look at another passage where the people of Jeremiah's day cry out for rescue without a spirit of honesty and repentance.

Read Jeremiah 4:31–5:3.

What are the people saying in 4:31b?

What is God's response to their cry? (5:1)

What does God accuse them of? (5:2-3)

Here we see the people crying out for help but still continuing in their sinful practices. The rest of Chapter 5 tells about their lust, lies, and treachery. But the main issue God brings out is their lies. When pride and selfishness are ruling our lives, we tell lies about ourselves that, in effect, cause us to tell lies about God. This is what leads us down the path to blaming God for the consequences of our bad decisions.

In *Till We Have Faces* by C. S. Lewis, a girl named Orual finds that she can't see God for who He is until she understands her own pride and sin. I know this has been true for me.

Here are some of the lies I sometimes tell about myself that cause me to tell lies about God:

> *When pride and selfishness are ruling our lives, we tell lies about ourselves that, in effect, cause us to tell lies about God.*

Lies About Myself ⟶	Lies About God ⟶	Truth
I deserve better. ⟶	God hasn't provided enough. ⟶	Philippians 4:19
I'm not qualified to do that. ⟶	God isn't able to do it through me. ⟶	Jeremiah 1
I don't need anybody. ⟶	God wants me to be independent. ⟶	Hebrews 10:24-25
My motives are right. ⟶	God says my heart is good. ⟶	Jeremiah 17:9
This is too little for God. ⟶	God doesn't care about details. ⟶	Psalm 37:23
This is too big for God. ⟶	My situation is too hard for God. ⟶	Jeremiah 32:17
My way is best. ⟶	I know better than God. ⟶	Jeremiah 6:16

These are just a few of the many distorted views that cause us to see God as unfair, unwilling, or unjust. In order to break free from these lies, we must see ourselves for who we really are, recognizing our flawed thinking and then applying God's Word of truth.

Identify three lies you tell about yourself that cause you to tell lies about God, writing each in the appropriate column below. Then look for truths in Scripture to refute these lies. Look in a concordance or do a keyword search in an online Bible. Begin committing these verses to memory.

Lie about yourself	Lie it causes you to tell about God	Scripture that refutes the lie
1.		
2.		
3.		

Crisis prayers often fall into the category of wanting rescue without repentance. "God, help me pass this test, and I'll be really good this week." "God, if you will just make my child better, we'll go to church more." "God, change my husband, and then I'll be a better wife." These are cries for rescue.

We all need rescuing, don't we? We may not have an army invading, but I haven't met many women with problem-free lives. We all cry out for rescue from time to time, asking for help with difficult relationships, marriage and/or parenting challenges, draining people, financial crises, work issues, and endless daily tasks. It's no wonder we are looking for some reprieve. God longs for us to cry out to Him for rescue; and when our struggles are a result of disobedience, He calls us to turn from our sin (repent) and walk in obedience to Him. God is always faithful to redirect us, rescuing us from a road of dangerous pitfalls.

> *God longs for us to cry out to Him for rescue; and when our struggles are a result of disobedience, He calls us to turn from our sin (repent) and walk in obedience to Him.*

Talk with God

What are you crying out to God to rescue you from right now? Perhaps there are some action steps of repentance that God is calling you to take that relate to your rescue. For example, you might need to make an attitude adjustment in a relationship. Or maybe there are nutrition, exercise, or sleep habits that need changing for your health, or prayer and Bible study habits that require attention for your spiritual well-being. Perhaps there are spending or saving habits you need to make to improve your finances. Or it could be that you need to offer a sacrifice of your time or provide more consistent discipline with your children. Listen to God now and be open to what He says. Make some notes below:

Now, to bring this week's focus to a close, ask yourself this question: Am I blaming God or others for my problems? Check one of the following blanks:

_____ YES – I need to stop blaming _____
for my problems.

Write a prayer of repentance and two action steps you will take to back up your words:

_____ NO – I don't blame others or God for the consequences of the choices I have made. I own my bad decisions and am trying to humbly follow God through my difficulties.

Write a prayer below, asking God to guard you against pride and keep you persevering in dependence on Him:

_____ NO – My current problems are not consequences of my decisions but are general results of living in a sinful, fallen world (cancer, job loss, illness, actions of others, and so on).

Write a prayer below, asking God to send His Holy Spirit to comfort you as you walk this tough path:

Read Through Jeremiah:

Read Jeremiah 43–44.

Digging Deeper

What is the equation E + R = O and how did it work out in the lives of the kings of Judah during Jeremiah's ministry? To consider how your current life events plus your personal responses impact your outcomes, go to AbingdonWomen.com/ Jeremiah and read Digging Deeper Week 5: "Royal Responsibility."

Video Viewer Guide

WEEK 5:
QUITTING THE BLAME GAME

Personal Responsibility

This is what the LORD says:

"Stop at the crossroads and look around.

    Ask for the old, godly way, and walk in it.

Travel its path, and you will find rest for your souls.

    But you reply, 'No, that's not the road we want!'"

Jeremiah 6:16 NLT

God's Prescription for Rest for Your Soul

1. _____ at the crossroads.

Why stop?

You've got to be careful you don't _____ someone else.

It's an opportunity for a _____ of _____.

2. _____ around.

We need to look _____ the surface and look _____ and see the situation from different people's point of view and from God's point of view.

3. _____ for the old, godly way.

The old, godly way is to love God with all your heart.

4. _____ the path.

VIDEO VIEWER GUIDE: WEEK 5

For the Kingdom of God is not just a lot of talk; it is living by God's power.

1 Corinthians 4:20 NLT

Side effects:

1. You're going to _____ _____ from the crowd.

2. You'll find great _____ in taking personal responsibility when you mess up.

Week 6
FINDING THE SOURCE
OF OUR HOPE
The Promised Messiah

Memory Verse

"For I know the plans I have for you," says the LORD. *"They are plans for good and not for disaster, to give you a future and a hope."*
                                                                              Jeremiah 29:11

Day 1: An Audience of One

"What will they think of me?" As women we can spend too much time worrying about what the spectators of our lives think about us. Consider these mental scenarios:

- Am I overdressed or underdressed? Do I fit in?
- Does my friend think my advice is good? Are my words what she wants to hear?
- If I'm too harsh with decision making/discipline, they will think I'm mean. If I'm too soft, they will think I'm a pushover.

These examples of self-talk reveal a woman who cares more about what others think than following the Holy Spirit's lead. We can all find ourselves here when we follow the path of fearing people more than God. In order to find the source of the hope we need to dare to have, we must worry less about what others think and more about obeying God. If we fear people more than God in the little things of life, such as how we are

We must worry less about what others think and more about obeying God.

dressed or what others think of our decision making or parenting, how will we tackle the real obstacles that threaten to take us down? When it comes to handling crises such as serious illness, job loss, or relationship breakdowns, the practice of living life to please God alone will get us through the tough times. Jeremiah has much to teach us about having an audience of one.

Read Jeremiah 2:17-20.

What was God doing for the people? (v. 17)

_____ **them on the way.**

What did they look to for security instead of their God? (v. 18)

Circle the two words used to describe what it is like for those who choose not to fear God:

"Your wickedness will punish you;
your backsliding will rebuke you.
Consider then and realize
how evil and bitter it is for you
when you forsake the LORD your God
and have no awe of me,"
declares the LORD, the LORD Almighty."
Jeremiah 2:19 NIV

"Don't call me Naomi," she responded. "Instead, call me Mara, for the Almighty has made life very bitter for me..."

Ruth 1:20

Evil and bitter don't top the list of my goals in life. Many translations use these two words because the meanings of the Hebrew words are so clear. The word used for evil is *ra'*, which means evil, very bad, or wicked[1]; and the word used for bitter is *mar*,[2] which is the root of the name Naomi gave herself after the death of her husbands and sons (Ruth 1:20). We never desire for these words to be associated with our lives, yet God describes the consequences of not fearing Him this way.

The people of Judah were trusting in political alliances with other nations even though God wanted to lead them. What are some modern-day things we trust instead of God when we are facing trouble—as individuals and as a nation?

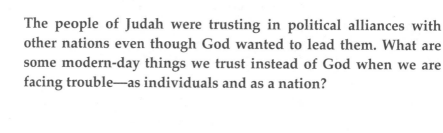

We may not face a Babylonian army, but we do have real fears about what could happen in the future. When challenges such as health issues, work problems or job loss, relational strains, financial worries, rebellious children, marital tension, and betrayal threaten to overpower us, where do we turn? Do we say we trust God with our mouths while our actions reveal otherwise?

What is your biggest fear right now? Go ahead and put words to it; God already knows.

What do your actions and thought life reveal about how consuming this fear is?

The antidote for the fear of people and circumstances is the fear of God. This is not the kind of fear that makes you want to hide in a closet from an abusive parent. It's a holy fear. As one source explains, "Such awe attracts you to God; it does not repel or leave you feeling shame. It makes you want to come to him and know him. When the fear of the Lord matures in you, Christ becomes irresistible."[3] As we know God more—His power, love, and ways—we will trust Him more with our fears. People and circumstances that used to scare us and keep us up at night will lose their hold over us in light of our relationship with the Lord of Heaven's Armies. When we follow Him closely, walk in obedience, and trust Him with our lives, we have nothing to fear.

> *When we follow Him closely, walk in obedience, and trust Him with our lives, we have nothing to fear.*

To make this even clearer, let's look at some narrative in Jeremiah and do some characterization. In a book filled with prophetic pronouncements, this is a rare instance of a real life story. As you read through these events, think of how each person or group of people displayed either fear of God or fear of people or circumstances with their words and/or actions.

On the next page, fill in the chart according to what you find in Jeremiah 26:1-24, noting how each displays fear of God and/or fear of people/circumstances. (Some display both kinds of fear while others display only one.)

Character(s)	Fear of God	Fear of People/Circumstances
Jeremiah		
Priests and Prophets		
Elders/ Wise Old Men		
Uriah, Son of Shemaiah		
King Jehoiakim		
Ahikam, Son of Shaphan		

Why was it easier for some of these people to fear people or circumstances than to trust God? (Try to put yourself in their shoes, asking, "What was it like? What made it so hard?")

What can make it hard for you to trust God when circumstances are difficult?

Another story in Jeremiah illustrates the importance of the fear of God contrasted with the fear of people or circumstances.

Read Jeremiah 36:23-24 in the margin. What is King Jehoiakim doing to the scrolls, and what has he failed to display?

Now read verses 30-31 in the margin. What does God say will happen to King Jehoiakim, and why?

What do you learn about the fear of God versus the fear of people/circumstances from this passage?

Whether it is little insecurities about what others think about your outfit or big decisions that tempt you to trust in things you can see and control rather than in God, fearing people and circumstances will always get us into big trouble and take us places we don't want to go. Living to please the spectators on the road of faith leads to manipulation, worry, and disappointment—and ultimately to discipline from a loving Father who wants to lead us back to Him as our source of hope. We need to evaluate what is bigger in our lives: people and circumstances, or God? When we live like Jeremiah, putting fear of God over fear of people or circumstances, the road is not problem-free, but it is blessed.

Read Through Jeremiah:

Read Jeremiah 45–46.

This topic hits home for me. I used to ride the approval roller coaster. When others praised and complimented me, my children, or my ministry, I soared. However, when people were critical of anything from my haircut to my husband, I spiraled downward into defeat and shame. Over the last year, through a gradual process of naming this issue, getting at the root of its pull on my heart, and devouring God's Word, God has freed me from my approval addiction. I now can say with the apostle Paul, "If I were still trying to please people, I would not be a servant of Christ" (Galatians 1:10c NIV). By teaching me to look for approval in the eyes of Him alone, God has blessed and freed my relationships with others. Though I must continually surrender this area of my life to Christ, today I am free to truly love those around me no matter if they throw me flowers or stones.

I'm praying a bouquet over you today! But when those stones come flying at you, as they inevitably will, remember there is one Spectator who is crazy about you. His name is Jesus, and He wants you to follow His path because He adores you and knows the dangers of the approval roller coaster. May you live today and every day for an audience of One!

Talk with God

Choose one (or more) of the following passages and prayerfully meditate on the words, asking God to speak to you about fearing Him.

Proverbs 1:7
Psalm 118:6
Psalm 147:11

Day 2: Good Plans Ahead

The movie *Soul Surfer* is about teen surfer Bethany Hamilton, who was attacked by a shark and lost her arm. In one scene of the movie, Bethany is attending a church youth group meeting where the youth leader shows them a couple of magnified images and asks them to guess what each object is. They come up with some funny answers. After showing each magnified image, the youth leader shows a photo that reveals the full object. The point she makes is that it can be hard to make sense of things when you're looking at them really closely; the same thing, she says, is true in life. Sometimes we need a different perspective.

We tend to live life "close up" without taking the time to back up and see what our circumstances look like from a year out, five years out, or in light of eternity. Today we will explore this theme by looking at perhaps the most-quoted verse from the Book of Jeremiah.

Read Jeremiah 29:10-14, and write verse 11 below:

Now, I don't want to burst the bubble of hope that this verse gives us, but we need to be careful not to overlook all that is going on here.

Go back and look at verse 10. What does God say is going to happen to them, and for how long, before these good plans happen?

Often it is our perspective that needs to change in order for us to see the good plans and the hope that God has for us now.

We like to think that this feel-good verse means God is going to change our circumstances right now. God is our hope, and He does have good plans for our future. However, for the people of Judah that hope included seventy more years of exile before circumstances changed. Often it is our perspective that needs to change in order for us to see the good plans and the hope that God has for us now.

Bethany Hamilton lost her arm in a shark attack, and that wasn't going to change. But she chose to get a new perspective on her difficult circumstance and see how God could use it. She put her trust in God, pursuing Him through her many trials, and she discovered that He was faithful and had good plans for her as a surfer even after a shark attack left her with only one arm.

Jeremiah 29:11 is not a promise to restore lost limbs or broken relationships, fill bank accounts, or make life problem-free. It is a promise to love and bless us even when times are tough.

Daniel was one of the people of Judah carried off in the early Babylonian invasion. He probably heard Jeremiah speak messages from God. Daniel set his mind to follow God faithfully, even when others were conforming

Fun Fact:

Some of His followers thought Jesus was Jeremiah returned to life. (See Matthew 16:14.)

to Babylonian culture. Though he remained in exile with his people in Babylon, God protected and blessed Daniel throughout those years of captivity.

Before they were taken captive, the people of Judah faced many other difficulties during the time of Jeremiah's prophecies. As we've learned through the weeks of our study, they suffered financial strain because they had to pay tribute to other nations, they endured corrupt leaders, and they lived in fear of Babylon—fears they saw come to pass. All of these difficulties left the people feeling desperate and unstable. At times I'm sure they found it difficult to believe that God's plans for them could be good in the midst of all these struggles.

When struggles come in your life, do you find it difficult to believe that God's plans for you are still good?

Jeremiah 29:11 is just one of many verses in Jeremiah's book that reveal God's heart to bring blessing even in difficult circumstances. Let's look at some other passages that reveal more of God's good plans for those who follow Him.

To see what God says about His ultimate plans for His people, read each Scripture and write what God promises to do for His people.

Jeremiah 30:7-11

Jeremiah 30:18-22

Jeremiah 31:1-14

Jeremiah 50:4-7

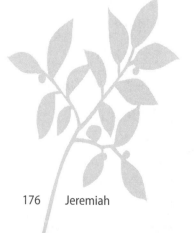

How do these promises that reveal God's heart to bless His people give you hope for your future? Put a star beside those that resonate with you personally.

God wants to bless us—to give us rest, hope, and peace. And these are good plans! However, because God knows that we cannot have these things apart from Him and that we are prone to wander, sometimes He allows difficult circumstances so that we will come back to Him. As C. S. Lewis wrote, "God whispers to us in our pleasures, speaks in our conscience, but shouts in our pain: it is His megaphone to rouse a deaf world."[4] Pain tends to get our attention when we stray.

God delights in providing for us, but He will not enable us in our sin. As a parent, I have a fuller understanding of this aspect of God's love. I want to spoil my children with every good thing in my power to give them. However, when I see them feeling or acting entitled, ungrateful, unhealthy, and ultimately miserable in their selfishness, I know that too much of a good thing has been detrimental. In those moments when their pain comes as a result of their own selfish choices, I still comfort them just as I do at other times, but I also allow natural and logical consequences to have their full effect so that my children can be motivated to refrain from repeating the same mistakes.

> *God delights in providing for us, but He will not enable us in our sin.*

God knows and understands our human state. He knows our bent toward sin. That's why He sent Jesus as a sacrifice, prophesying about Him through Jeremiah so many years before His coming. Ultimately, God's best plan for all who follow Him is spending eternity with Him. While in this life there is much suffering, in the next there will be no tears. Even if the world crumbles around us or we must face many years in a difficult circumstance, we can know with confidence that God's plans are good because one day we will see Him face to face. Talk about a future and a hope!

If you are still struggling to believe in God's good plans for you, end your time in God's Word today by looking up the following verses to see what the Bible says you have in store:

Romans 8:37

Read Through Jeremiah:

Read Jeremiah 47–48.

1 Corinthians 13:12-13

1 Corinthians 15:54-57

1 John 4:4

Revelation 19:6-7

How do these truths increase your faith in the God of hope?

Talk with God

Spend some time in God's presence, listening for what good, hopeful things He wants to speak over your life. Then praise Him for what He has planned for you!

To guard against those times when life seems devoid of hope, choose one of the New Testament Scriptures listed above and meditate on it now, beginning to hide the words in your heart. After your prayer time, write the Scripture on an index card and carry it with you so that you can meditate on this promise whenever you need a hopeful reminder that God has good plans for you.

Day 3: Hope That Brings Us Back

During the weeks of our study in Jeremiah, we have seen God's repeated declarations of intent to exile His people from their land because of their habitual, unrepentant sin. We've seen that sin separates us from God, driving a wedge in the close relationship He desires to have with us. Today we will examine more closely God's heart that always longs to draw us back.

To get a fuller understanding of God's hopeful plan against a backdrop of idolatry, disobedience, and hard hearts, let's journey from the days of Jeremiah back to the days of the United Kingdom in Israel. Bear with me for this brief history review; I promise it has significant implications for our focus today on God's longing to draw us back to Him.

Kings first began ruling Israel in 1050 B.C. when the people begged God for a king so that they could be like other nations. This was roughly five hundred years before Jeremiah's proclamations from God. God warned the people against wanting a monarchy, but He gave them Saul as their first king after their constant pestering. (Our God doesn't force His way on us. Sometimes He lets us learn through experience that His way is best.)

After Saul, David became king and ruled as "a man after [God's] own heart" (1 Samuel 13:14). During David's reign, we see a clear picture of God's desire to look for ways to bring us back to Him when we have been disobedient. In 2 Samuel 14:14, we find these words, "But God does not just sweep life away; instead, he devises ways to bring us back when we have been separated from him." After David's death, his son Solomon became king and built the Temple. In Solomon's prayer of dedication of the Temple found in 1 Kings 8, we find a reference to the days of Jeremiah that reveals God's desire to draw His people back.

Read 1 Kings 8:46-51. What are the people to do when they find themselves in exile?

The hope we see in these verses looks something like this to me:

God knows our tendency to sin.
He gives us an opportunity to repent.
He forgives us and restores us when we turn to Him.

Even here in the Old Testament we see the beauty of God's gospel. We resemble the people in Jeremiah's day more than we care to admit. We worship counterfeits, struggle with a lack of listening, suffer from hardheartedness, and often blame others when we mess up. First Kings 8:46 says, "And who has never sinned?" We all struggle daily with the "sin disease" that wants to kill our soul. Yet our God longs for us to return to Him and offers us a way back. He says we are to confess and repent.

> *We all struggle daily with the "sin disease" that wants to kill our soul. Yet our God longs for us to return to Him and offers us a way back. He says we are to confess and repent.*

What sinful habits or practices are keeping you at a distance from a close relationship with your God right now? You can write them in code if you want, using only the first letter of each word.

Using your list as a guide, take a minute to confess and repent right now. Lay each sin before God, asking Him to help you turn from your sin and toward Him through the hope you have in Christ.

Now let's continue our journey through history. King Solomon's son Rehoboam inherited only the lands of Judah and Benjamin, and the other ten tribes of Israel split off under Jeroboam's leadership to form the nation of Israel. So Judah and Israel became two separate nations that often fought each other. Israel abandoned their God, and God sent many prophets with His messages of repentance (such as, Elijah, Elisha, Hosea, and Amos). Once again we see God's heart to draw His people back. Finally, after their refusal to repent, the people of Israel were carried off into captivity by Assyria in 722 B.C.

Unfortunately, the people of Judah did not learn from Israel's punishment. They had a few godly kings who led some revivals, but by Jeremiah's day, wickedness and sin had a foothold in the people's heart. At that time God sent Jeremiah to call them to repentance—yet again demonstrating His longing to draw His people back—but they wouldn't listen. So in 586 B.C., Babylon invaded and destroyed Jerusalem.

It may seem pretty bleak for God's people at this point. After all, where is the hope in exile, destruction, and punishment?

Have you ever felt hopeless in *your* circumstances? Tell of a time when it seemed that nothing good could come out of your trials.

Even in the midst of the promised punishment for sin, we see God's longing for His people. You see, God offers hope for a remnant who are willing to follow Him. This remnant is not a leftover piece of fabric! The *Holman Bible Dictionary* defines a remnant as "something left over, especially the righteous people of God after divine judgment."[5] The concept of remnant is found throughout the pages of Scripture, reminding us that even in times of God's judgment, He offers hope to any who will return to Him. We see Noah's family left as a remnant after the flood. When Elijah claims to be the only follower of God left, God reminds him

> *Even in times of God's judgment, He offers hope to any who will return to Him.*

that a remnant of seven thousand remain faithful (1 Kings 19:10-18). As one source points out, "It is in the [Old Testament] prophets that the remnant theme flowers into full blossom. The Hebrew words for 'remnant' (she'ar, she'erit) occur over one hundred times in the prophetic books."[6] Jeremiah also predicts a future day when God will bring His people back to their Promised Land.

Let's look to Jeremiah's words for mentions of God's hope offered to the remnant that will obey Him.

What does God say about His remnant of followers in these passages in Jeremiah?

5:10, 18

23:3-4

50:17-20

> *"But I will gather together the remnant of my flock from the countries where I have driven them. I will bring them back to their own sheepfold, and they will be fruitful and increase in number.*
>
> *Then I will appoint responsible shepherds who will care for them, and they will never be afraid again. Not a single one will be lost or missing. I, the LORD, have spoken!*
>
> **Jeremiah 23:3-4**

God often speaks of the remnant of His people with words of hope and compassion. They have been through a lot of difficulty, which has left them humble and ready to obey. These are the people who have learned to trust in Him through their struggles. Here we see God gathering His people with promises of rest, peace, and forgiveness.

How do these promises offer you hope for those times when your sin causes you to feel isolated from God?

Unfortunately, not everyone chooses to practice humility and to trust in God during tough times. So we find another remnant in Jeremiah that did not learn the lesson of repentance after the catastrophe of exile (Jeremiah 42:18-20; 44:12-14; 47:4-5). God will use anything to bring us near to Him, but He will not force our hand. Although the remnant mentioned in Scripture is usually connected with repentance and hope,

there is another remnant made up of those who endure the Lord's discipline and still insist on going their own way. Because of the hardness of their hearts and their refusal to turn to God, the plans God has for this unrepentant remnant are more discipline, not peace. This makes me want to learn my lessons quickly so that I can get to the hopeful part!

Because God loves us and knows what is best for us, He calls us to give up control and follow Him wholeheartedly. He also asks us to be daring with hope. Sometimes that means being a remnant of only one. Jeremiah knew what this felt like.

> *Because God loves us and knows what is best for us, He calls us to give up control and follow Him wholeheartedly. He also asks us to be daring with hope.*

In Jeremiah 15:18-21, we find Jeremiah complaining to the Lord about his suffering. Read these verses and answer the following questions.

Jeremiah complains that God's help seems "as uncertain as a seasonal brook, like a spring that has gone dry" (v. 18). He is basically saying to God, "Sometimes it seems like You are here, and sometimes it seems like You aren't." Have you ever felt that way?

What does God call Jeremiah to do? (v. 19)

What does God promise to Jeremiah even when he must stand alone? (vv. 20-21)

God reassured Jeremiah that he could stand alone; God would rescue and protect him. Like Jeremiah, even when we must stand alone as the only one in our family, our friend group, or even our church who dares to hope in God in tough times, God promises to be our Protector. We can trust God, even when we don't "feel" that we can.

For us, standing alone doesn't usually mean preaching a message of surrender, as it did for Jeremiah. When I think back on times when I had to stand alone, I recall being teased in high school because I chose to be morally pure. Through the years I have been blessed to have friends in the body of Christ who have stood with me at different times for different reasons; however, there have been a few very lonely times when even close friends couldn't understand some of my decisions. It has been those times, through many tears and heartbreak, that a sweet closeness with Christ has sustained me even when I felt alone.

I've read the stories of many missionaries, and I've found that the real movers and shakers for God—saints such as Gladys Aylward, Hudson Taylor, George Mueller—faced many people who questioned their desire to follow Christ in the ways that they did. They had to stand alone. They were discouraged, misunderstood, and laughed at—not only by the world but also by people in the church—for doing daring things in obedience to Christ. Though none of them had to bury underwear, hang out in a muddy cistern, or wear a wooden yoke in the streets as Jeremiah did, they each had to take bold stands in the name of Christ.

Though we must always be sure that what we feel called to do is a leading of the Holy Spirit, we must be obedient to a call we are certain is from God even if others believe it is crazy, dangerous, or radical. We must be willing to stand alone for God, trusting He will protect and sustain us.

> *We must be willing to stand alone for God, trusting He will protect and sustain us.*

When have you had to stand alone for God? When have you been excluded, gossiped about, questioned, or humiliated because of your values, beliefs, choices, or actions?

How did God sustain you through this time?

Whether we're a remnant of one or many, the hopeful message of the remnant is that God softens and teaches us through every trial or challenge

> ***Read Through Jeremiah:***
>
> *Read Jeremiah 49–50.*

so that we will know Him in a more intimate way. He is always devising ways to bring us back to Him or draw us even closer. Even in those times when we choose to go our own way, He gives us opportunities to recognize our sin so that we may turn from it and toward our God. He is always ready to forgive and restore our relationship. There is no situation or sin problem that is hopeless. The God of hope longs for us to walk closely with Him.

Tomorrow we'll explore Jeremiah's messages about Jesus—our ultimate Hope for finding our way back to God!

Talk with God

Recall some sweet fellowship you have enjoyed with Christ during a difficult time. Thank Him for the blessing of that closeness and intimacy. Then offer thanks for any current trial or challenge you may be experiencing, acknowledging it as an opportunity to learn and grow and draw even closer to Him.

Day 4: The Promised Messiah

Six hundred years before Mary would be visited by an angel, God promised us a Messiah through the prophet Jeremiah. Talk about *hope*!

We've seen Jeremiah repeating phrases of importance throughout his book. Here are a few examples of repetition that we've studied in previous weeks:

- The leaders offer "superficial treatments for [God's] people's mortal wound." (Jeremiah 6:14 and 8:11)
- Three times in one chapter Jeremiah emphasizes that Baruch recorded the words Jeremiah spoke that came from the Lord. (Jeremiah 36:4, 8, 32)
- God speaks of the people's abandonment of Him as the fountain of living water. (Jeremiah 2:13 and 17:13)

These are just three of the many times that God uses repetition to get our attention throughout Jeremiah's prophecy. It's no surprise, then, that God would have him repeat truths about the coming Messiah for emphasis.

Fun Fact:

"Days are coming" is a messianic formula used more than a dozen times in the Book of Jeremiah.

Both Jeremiah 23:5-8 and 33:14-18 describe the One who is coming to save God's people in the future. Pick one of these two almost identical passages to read; then write three characteristics of the promised One below:

1.

2.

3.

The name used for God in both texts is "The LORD Is Our Righteousness," *Jehovah Tsidkenu*.[7] We've seen over and over in Jeremiah that we can't have righteousness on our own. Jeremiah 17:9 reminds us that our hearts are desperately wicked. God was forthtelling the future in which He would send a Messiah to be righteousness for us.

The New Testament sheds further light on what Jeremiah's words promised.

> *"The human heart is the most deceitful of all things, and desperately wicked. Who really knows how bad it is?"*
>
> **Jeremiah 17:9**

Read the verses below and circle words or phrases that describe how Christ's righteousness benefits us as believers:

For the sin of this one man, Adam, caused death to rule over many. But even greater is God's wonderful grace and his gift of righteousness, for all who receive it will live in triumph over sin and death through this one man, Jesus Christ.

Yes, Adam's one sin brings condemnation for everyone, but Christ's one act of righteousness brings a right relationship with God and new life for everyone.

Romans 5:17-18

For they don't understand God's way of making people right with himself. Refusing to accept God's way, they cling to their own way of getting right with God by trying to keep the law. For Christ has already accomplished the purpose for which the law was given. As a result, all who believe in him are made right with God.

Romans 10:3-4

So we are Christ's ambassadors; God is making his appeal through us. We speak for Christ when we plead, "Come back to God!" For God made Christ, who never sinned, to be the offering for our sin, so that we could be made right with God through Christ.

2 Corinthians 5:20-21

How would you explain in one sentence how we are made right with God?

Did you catch it? God makes us right with Him through Christ. Even as Jeremiah prophesied, God knew that He would send Christ to be our righteousness. He knew our need for a Savior, and He offered hope to the remnant that the Messiah would come one day.

How awesome for us that we know that Jesus has already come and paid the penalty for our sin. Our constant bent toward foolishness and our desperately wicked hearts are constant reminders of our need to depend on Him. His righteousness is part of the armor of God given to protect our hearts.

Stand firm then, with the belt of truth buckled around your waist, with the breastplate of righteousness in place.

Ephesians 6:14 NIV

According to Ephesians 6:14 in the margin, which piece of armor is God's righteousness?

Yes, His righteousness is the breastplate that protects us from thinking we can be righteous on our own. I don't think it's a coincidence that righteousness is what God gave us to protect our hearts!

We battle guilt, fear, and condemnation from the enemy, who tempts us to sin and then throws our failure in our faces. God wants us to follow Him wholeheartedly, and when we inevitably mess up, He calls us to turn to Him in repentance rather than run from Him in shame. When we understand that He sent Christ to be our righteousness so that we can be made right with Him regardless of our screwups, it protects our hearts from shame.

What guilt and shameful lies has the enemy been aiming at your heart recently?

Put on the breastplate of righteousness right now through prayer, and praise God that He sent Jesus to be your righteousness to free you from guilt and shame. Pray something like this:

God, thank you for the armor. You know these battles I am fighting. Place the breastplate of your righteousness over my heart right now. Help me to walk in the freedom you purchased for me on the cross. Let the enemy's attempts to attack me with shame and guilt bounce right off your strong armor that protects my heart. Amen.

Not only did Jeremiah teach about Christ coming to be our righteousness, He also spoke clearly about the new covenant that would come to make the way for us to be right with God. Jeremiah 31:31-37 gives a snapshot of a day in the future when there would be a new covenant, and the Ten Commandments would be more than just laws written in stone.

What would be a sign of the new covenant? (v. 33)

What does God say He will do in regard to our sins? (v. 34)

How likely is God to reject His people? (vv. 36-37)

What an amazing thought! God will do away with gravity before He will abandon us!

How does this hopeful message encourage you—especially knowing that we are living under the new covenant?

In the Old Testament, people were saved by faith in the coming Messiah. They didn't know His name or exactly how the prophecies would be fulfilled, but it was their faith in Messiah that made them right with God. The Temple sacrifices, priesthood, and even the Temple itself were all a foretaste of what would be fulfilled in Christ. In the New Testament we see Christ identified as our High Priest (Hebrews 4:14) as well as the final sacrifice for sin (Hebrews 10:1-10). In Hebrews 10:9 we read this about Christ: "Then he said, 'Look, I have come to do your will.' He cancels the first covenant in order to put the second into effect."

God gave those living under the old covenant (Old Testament) glimpses ahead to the Messiah in whom they were placing their faith and hope. They didn't know about the cross or the nails or the crown of thorns, and they did not fully understand how this Messiah would rescue them; but they knew they needed saving.

If we were to draw a picture to represent salvation for those living before and after the cross, it would look something like this:

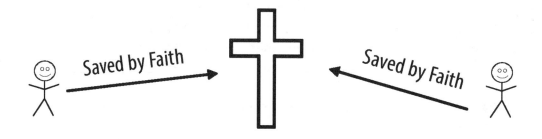

The Lord tells us that He is the true hope of Israel (Jeremiah 17:13). Jesus is the ultimate fulfillment of that hope. He came to give us life, to be our righteousness, to be the bridge from sinful humanity to a holy God.

> *Though our sin separates us from God, He longs to be close to us. He wants us to know Him. So He sent Christ, His Son, as the perfect sacrifice to take the payment for all our sins upon Himself.*

Though our sin separates us from God, He longs to be close to us. He wants us to know Him. So He sent Christ, His Son, as the perfect sacrifice to take the payment for all our sins upon Himself. He made a new covenant so that when we accept Christ's payment on the cross by faith, we can have a relationship with a holy God. Now when God the Father looks down on us, He sees us through the lens of Christ's sacrifice. He sees us as righteous because of what Christ has done for us. This frees us from our shame, our guilt, and our fear.

I understood this for the first time as a nine-year-old girl. I remember watching my brother and sister fighting on the porch through the screen door, thinking, "They have already decided to follow Christ." I purposed in my heart that I would not decide to follow Christ until I could be good all the time. I knew I wasn't ready. Then a few months later in Sunday school, a sweet teacher explained to me that I didn't have to clean myself up for God. I just had to come to Him and recognize my sin because I would never get rid of it on my own. For the first time I understood that I didn't have to be "good enough" for God; I only needed to accept His payment for my sin on the cross so that He could become "The Lord Is My Righteousness." This began my journey of walking with Christ.

Fun Fact:

Jeremiah enjoyed free and open conversation with God.

At times I still struggle with seeking approval from God based on my performance. When I'm doing well in obeying God, a tendency for pride creeps in, and when I fail, shame often comes knocking at my door. So when I sense I am heading down this path of performance-based acceptance, I stop and remind myself of God's grace through Christ.

I like what Philip Yancey has written about grace: "Grace means there is nothing I can do to make God love me more, and nothing I can do to make God love me less. It means that I, even I who deserve the opposite, am invited to take my place at the table in God's family."[8] Christ's sacrifice made it possible for each of us to be at the table as part of God's family. Jeremiah looked forward to this new covenant with anticipation. We look backward to Christ's finished work on the cross with gratefulness. Through faith in the revelation God has provided, we trust Him to be our righteousness.

> "Grace means there is nothing I can do to make God love me more, and nothing I can do to make God love me less."[8]
> —Philip Yancey

Talk with God

Reflect on the truth that there is nothing you can do to make God love you more and nothing you can do to make God love you less. Talk with God about how this gives you hope, thanking Him for His amazing grace through Christ. Write below a prayer of thanksgiving to God for sending Christ on your behalf:

Day 5: Full Access

I can't believe this is our last day together in the Book of Jeremiah. It has been quite a journey as we've studied Jeremiah's messages about surrender, idolatry, listening, heart issues, personal responsibility, and hope in the promised Messiah. We will continue to see hope in the prophecies about Christ as we look at words Jeremiah wrote that went far beyond the scope of Judah's return from captivity in Babylon. Through Jeremiah God spoke of a day of restoration, reassuring us that His discipline doesn't last forever. He uses every bit of it to bring about a singleness of heart and mind that realizes God alone is worthy of our complete trust.

Begin by writing the eleven power-packed words of Jeremiah 32:38 below:

Our hope rests in this statement. No matter the outcome of any election, the heights and depths of our economics, or the opinions of others, each of us can be God's woman. In an unstable world, He will always be our God.

In the next verses, God goes on to make even more promises to those who choose to follow Him.

And I will give them one heart and one purpose: to worship me forever, for their own good and for the good of all their descendants.

And I will make an everlasting covenant with them: I will never stop doing good for them. I will put a desire in their hearts to worship me, and they will never leave me.

I will find joy doing good for them and will faithfully and wholeheartedly replant them in this land.

Jeremiah 32:39-41

Read Jeremiah 32:39-41 in the margin and write what God says He will give in each verse:

v. 39

v. 40

v. 41

Jesus fulfills all of these promises. He ushered in the everlasting covenant through His sacrifice. He made the way for us to be God's people through His shed blood on the cross. Then He rose again to new life, offering us resurrection power to help us live victoriously. He even finds "joy [in] doing good" for us (v. 41). He longs for us to put our hope in Him so that we can have a close relationship with Him.

How do these words of blessing from your God bring you hope today?

What is holding you back from fully believing these promises and applying them in your current circumstances?

Part of this new everlasting covenant that Jeremiah foretold concerns our direct access to God. We've read about the priests and the sacrifices they offered in the Temple throughout Jeremiah's prophecy. In Chapter 33, Jeremiah speaks about a line of kings and priests that will come from David's descendants.

What does Jeremiah 33:18 (in the margin) say there will always be?

> *"And there will always be Levitical priests to offer burnt offerings and grain offerings and sacrifices to me."*
>
> **Jeremiah 33:18**

The author of the New Testament book of Hebrews knew these prophecies of Jeremiah well. In Hebrews 10:8-18, we get a clear picture of how Christ fulfills Jeremiah's prophecy. The writer even quotes directly from Jeremiah's book.

What does Hebrews 10:12 (in the margin) tell us about Christ's death on the cross?

> *But our High Priest offered himself to God as a single sacrifice for sins, good for all time. Then he sat down in the place of honor at God's right hand.*
>
> **Hebrews 10:12**

What does this mean for us? Through Christ, we can come directly to our God. We don't need to offer animals or go through a priest.

Think about this: if you could have access to a great Christian leader in our day, who would it be? Now imagine if that person gave you his or her personal phone number and said, "Call or text me anytime you have questions or are struggling. I will pray for you, counsel you, and encourage you." Would you lose the number and never contact the person, or would you call often to build a relationship?

The question facing us is this: are we taking full advantage of our full access to the One who is our source of hope? Others can help us, but that doesn't even compare to what God offers us through a relationship with Him. Although sin separates us from God, Christ restores our relationship through His sacrifice on the cross. So now we can enjoy friendship with a Holy God. Romans 5:10-11 says, "For since our friendship with God was restored by the death of his Son while we were still his enemies, we will certainly be saved through the life of his Son. So now we can rejoice in our wonderful new relationship with God because our Lord Jesus Christ has made us friends of God." Through Christ you hold a backstage VIP pass to the God of the universe! He waits with joy to help you through the storms of life.

> *Through Christ you hold a backstage VIP pass to the God of the universe! He waits with joy to help you through the storms of life.*

What can you do to take even greater advantage of this access to God that you have in Jesus?

Jeremiah understood the importance of placing His hope and confidence in God—not just occasionally, but daily. We get a peek into Jeremiah's heart through his prayers. He not only wrote the book of the Bible containing the most words, but he also penned the Book of Lamentations, which follows the Book of Jeremiah. It contains his laments. A "lament" is a passionate expression of sorrow; it involves looking back on grief or devastation and shedding tears. In the midst of Lamentations is a famous text that cannot be overlooked when talking about hope in the midst of despair.

Read Lamentations 3:21-27. What do you learn in these verses about this God that you have full access to through Christ?

Now make note of what our responses should be according to verses 24-27.

God has not abandoned us. When it seems like all hope is lost, He is still our God. He has good plans for us. Those plans involve us living with purpose. Instead of running through life trying to get it all done, we need to slow down and live with care. We need to remember to hope—knowing that we have a Redeemer who has paid for all our sins. He has good works planned in advance for us. He wants us to live in the light of His return. In other words, the fact that Jesus will come again should affect the way I live today, tomorrow, and the next day. It gives meaning and urgency for pursuing a close relationship with Him.

> *God has not abandoned us. When it seems like all hope is lost, He is still our God.*

As we saw yesterday, God is more apt to forget about the laws of nature (such as gravity) than He is to forget about us. He sees us. He wants us to know Him intimately. He is even willing to allow difficulty in our lives to bring us back into relationship with Him when we stray. He wants us to put away our idols, cling to Him like underwear, get on the right path, and stop blaming others when we mess up. His plans are not to harm us but to give us a future and a hope (Jeremiah 29:11). Let's humble ourselves before our God and live like He makes a difference in our lives.

The following verse held great relevance for the people of Judah, but it has real application in our lives as well.

Read Jeremiah 51:5 below and write your name in the blank, replacing "Israel and Judah":

"For the LORD of Heaven's Armies

    has not abandoned _____.

He is still [your] God,

    even though [your] land was filled with sin

    against the Holy One of Israel."

No matter what is happening in your life right now, God has not abandoned you. He is your only real source of hope. You must choose daily to dare to hope in Him alone, no matter what this unstable world throws your way. I pray that you will!

Read Through Jeremiah:

Read Jeremiah 51:33-64.

As we end our study in Jeremiah, take a few moments to review our six themes one last time:

Raising the White Flag (Surrender)

Recognizing Counterfeits and the Real Deal (Idolatry)

Opening Our Ears (Listening)

Staying Spiritually Sensitive (Heart Issues)

Quitting the Blame Game (Personal Responsibility)

Finding the Source of Our Hope (The Promised Messiah)

Circle the theme above that has resonated most strongly in your heart and mind as we have studied together.

Are there practical steps you need to take in order to let the truths we've explored related to this theme sink in more deeply? Check all that apply, making notes in the space provided:

_____ Are there verses you need to memorize?

_____ Are there sins you need to confess to God—and perhaps someone who will hold you accountable?

_____ Are there spiritual disciplines you need to institute in your prayer and study life?

_____ Are there bold steps you need to take to smash idols in your life?

_____ Do you have thought patterns you need to take captive?

_____ Are you allowing God to do the painful work of softening a hard heart?

_____ Are there people in your life God wants you to proclaim His message of surrender to?

_____ Other things God's Spirit is bringing to mind:

Thanks so much for hanging in there with me for these six weeks of study. I have prayed for you all along the way, and our time together has been sweet. Though our journey has come to an end, our individual journeys continue. My prayer is that we will continue to be daring with hope—no matter what may happen in our own personal struggles, our country, or our world. We can dare to hope because we have found the Source of our hope.

Even if your circumstances haven't budged an inch, or perhaps have intensified, I pray that your hope has grown because of God's steadfast love and new mercies. Jeremiah dared to hope even when he found that all that he'd hoped for from the Lord was lost (Lamentations 3:18). Throughout the writing of this study I have seen my twin daughters struggling with alopecia. One has lost all of her hair and the other has begun losing her hair as well. Some days I have felt like I was in the bottom of a pit. Yet at the same time, I have found that my greatest struggles have become some of God's greatest triumphs in my life. He has used the trials to draw me nearer to Him. I pray that this has been true for you as well and that we can continue to dare to hope through whatever tomorrow may bring.

Talk with God

Ask God to make clear the main take-away for you from the Book of Jeremiah. Be ready to share in your last group session a brief summary of God's work in your life over the past six sessions. Make some notes below:

Digging Deeper

Why has Jeremiah been referred to as a "Christ type"? What significance does that have for us in our study of Jeremiah's message? To see what Jeremiah and Jesus have in common, check out Digging Deeper Week 6: "J²" at AbingdonWomen.com/Jeremiah.

Video Viewer Guide

WEEK 6:
FINDING THE SOURCE OF OUR HOPE

The Promised Messiah

Jeremiah is called the most _____-_____ of the prophets.

- Both wept over the city of Jerusalem.
- Both were taken to Egypt against their will.
- Both were rejected in their own hometowns.
- Both had an authenticity when speaking to God.
- The big difference: Jeremiah was a sinner; Jesus was sinless.

Jeremiah referred to the Messiah as "The LORD Is Our Righteousness" (Jeremiah 23:5-6; Jeremiah 33:15-16).

What are we saved from?

1. Justification – Saved from the _____ of our sin.

2. Sanctification – Saved from the _____ of sin in our lives.

God is more concerned about our _____ than our _____.

To all who mourn in Israel,

    he will give a crown of _____ for ashes,

a joyous _____ instead of mourning,

    festive _____ instead of despair.

In their righteousness, they will be like great oaks

    that the LORD has planted for his own glory.

Isaiah 61:3 NLT

3. Glorification – Saved from the very _____ of sin.

I cry out, "My splendor is gone!

  Everything I had hoped for from the LORD is lost!"

The thought of my _____ and homelessness

  is bitter beyond words.

I will never forget this awful time,

as I grieve over my loss.

Yet I still dare to _____

  when I remember this:

The faithful love of the LORD never ends!

  His mercies never cease.

Great is his _____;

  his mercies begin afresh each morning.

                    Lamentations 3:18-23 NLT

"For I know the plans I have for you," declares the Lord, "plans to prosper you and not to harm you, plans to give you hope and a future."

                                   Jeremiah 29:11 NIV

Notes

Introduction

1. Francis Schaeffer, *Death in the City* (Wheaton, IL: Crossway Books, 2002), 33.

Week 1

1. Frank E. Gaebelein, *The Expositor's Bible Commentary*, Volume 6 (Grand Rapids, MI: Zondervan, 1986), 358.
2. Schaeffer, 33.
3. Jennifer Degler, What's Wrong with Nice Girls, June 5, 2011, http://lifetoday.org/connect/words-of-life/whats-wrong-with-nice-girls/
4. Craig Groeschel, *The Christian Atheist: Believing in God but Living As If He Doesn't Exist* (Grand Rapids, MI: Zondervan, 2010), 135.
5. Gaebelein, 358.
6. *The Bible Knowledge Commentary: Old Testament* (Cedar Rapids, IA: Laridian, 2010), PocketBible for Windows software.
7. "Shuwb," http://www.biblestudytools.com/lexicons/hebrew/kjv/shuwb.html.
8. "Batach," http://biblehub.com/hebrew/983.htm.

Week 2

1. "Mowqesh," http://www.biblestudytools.com/lexicons/hebrew/kjv/mowqesh.html.
2. John MacArthur, *The MacArthur Bible Commentary* (Nashville, TN: Thomas Nelson, 2005), 849.
3. Timothy Keller, *Counterfeit Gods: The Empty Promises of Money, Sex, and Power, and the Only Hope that Matters* (New York: Penguin, 2009), xvii.
4. Keller, *Counterfeit Gods*, 23-24.
5. Keller, *Counterfeit Gods*, 17.
6. Elisabeth Elliot, *Through Gates of Splendor* (Peabody, MA: Hendrickson, 1996), 173.

7. Today, around 21,000 children died around the world," Anup Shah, *Global Issues*, last modified September 24, 2011, http://www.globalissues.org/article/715/today-21000-children-died-around-the-world.

8. Mail Online, Monday, March 10, 2014, http://www.dailymail.co.uk/health/article-1269088/Bowel-cancer-Doctors-told-Vicky-IBS--fact-tumour-size-orange.html.

Week 3

1. "Shama," http://www.biblestudytools.com/lexicons/hebrew/kjv/shama.html.

2. "The Shema—Hear, O Israel, the LORD is our God; the LORD is one," http://www.hebrew4christians.com/Scripture/Torah/The_Shema/the_shema.html.

3. Gaebelein, 357.

4. "Yatsar," http://www.biblestudytools.com/lexicons/hebrew/kjv/yatsar-2.html.

5. "Lord Sabaoth," http://www.biblegateway.com/resources/dictionaries/dict_meaning.php?source=1&wid=T0003169.

6. MacArthur, 303.

7. Warren W. Wiersbe. *Be Amazed: Restoring an Attitude of Wonder and Worship* (Wheaton, IL: Victor Books, 1996), 176.

8. "Dabaq," http://www.biblestudytools.com/lexicons/hebrew/kjv/dabaq.html.

9. Jack R. Lundbom, *The Anchor Bible, Jeremiah 1-20* (New York: Doubleday, 1999), 669.

10. Ralph Gower, *The New Manners & Customs of Bible Times* (Chicago: Moody Publishers, 2005), 328.

11. Gaebelein, 524.

Week 4

1. "Shama," http://www.biblestudytools.com/lexicons/hebrew/kjv/shama.html.

2. "Chaciyd," http://www.biblestudytools.com/lexicons/hebrew/kjv/chaciyd.html.

3. Gaebelein, 369.

4. Marilyn Hontz, *Shame Lifter: Replacing Your Fears and Tears with Forgiveness, Truth, and Hope* (Carol Stream, IL: Tyndale, 2009), xviii.

Week 5

1. "My Hope Is Built," words by Edward Mote, 1834, *The United Methodist Hymnal* (Nashville, TN: The United Methodist Publishing House, 1989), 368, refrain.

2. *Harper's Bible Dictionary* (New York: Harper & Row, 1985), 178.

3. *The Rookie*, http://www.imdb.com/title/tt0265662/quotes.

4. Gower, 215.

5. Philip J. King, *Jeremiah: An Archaeological Companion* (Louisville: Westminster/John Knox Press, 1993), 12.

Week 6

1. "Ra'," http://www.biblestudytools.com/lexicons/hebrew/nas/ra.html.

2. "Mar," http://www.biblestudytools.com/lexicons/hebrew/nas/mar.html.

3. Edward T. Welch, *When People Are Big and God Is Small* (Phillipsburg, NJ: P&R Publishing, 1997), 123.

4. C. S. Lewis, *The Problem of Pain* (San Francisco: Harper Collins, 1940), 91.

5. Chad Brand, Charles Draper, and Archie England, general editors, *Holman Illustrated Bible Dictionary* (Nashville, TN: Holman Bible Publishers, 2003), 1374.

6. Tremper Longman III, *The Baker Illustrated Bible Dictionary* (Grand Rapids, MI: Baker Books, 2013), 1409.

7. "Jehovah Tsidkenu," http://www.biblestudytools.com/dictionary/jehovah-tsidkenu/.

8. Philip Yancey, *What's So Amazing About Grace?* (Grand Rapids, MI: Zondervan, 1997), 71.

Memory Verses

Cut out your memory verses and carry them with you for easy reflection or post them in a convenient location where you can see them daily.

Note: The following verses are from The New Living Translation. If you prefer, feel free to choose a different translation for memorization.

Week 1

*When I discovered your words,
I devoured them.
    They are my joy and my heart's
    delight,
for I bear your name,
    O LORD God of Heaven's Armies.*
                    Jeremiah 15:16

Week 2

*Idols are worthless; they are ridiculous
lies!
    On the day of reckoning they will
    all be destroyed.
But the God of Israel is no idol!
    He is the Creator of everything
    that exists,
including Israel, his own special
possession.
    The LORD of Heaven's Armies is
    his name!*
                    Jeremiah 10:15-16

Week 3

*"Ask me and I will tell you remarkable
secrets you do not know about things
to come."*
                    Jeremiah 33:3

Week 4

*"The human heart is the most deceitful of
all things,
    and desperately wicked.
    Who really knows how bad it is?
But I, the LORD, search all hearts
    and examine secret motives.
I give all people their due rewards,
    according to what their actions
    deserve."*
                    Jeremiah 17:9-10

Week 5

*This is what the LORD says:
"Don't let the wise boast in their wisdom,
    or the powerful boast in their power,
    or the rich boast in their riches.
But those who wish to boast
    should boast in this alone:
that they truly know me and understand
that I am the LORD. . . ."*
                    Jeremiah 9:23-24

Week 6

*"For I know the plans I have for you,"
says the LORD. "They are plans for good
and not for disaster, to give you a future
and a hope."*
                    Jeremiah 29:11

Week 1

When I discovered your words, I devoured them.
  They are my joy and my heart's delight,
for I bear your name,
  O Lord God of Heaven's Armies.

Jeremiah 15:16

Week 2

Idols are worthless; they are ridiculous lies!
  On the day of reckoning they will all be
  destroyed.
But the God of Israel is no idol!
  He is the Creator of everything that exists,
including Israel, his own special possession.
  The Lord of Heaven's Armies is his name!

Jeremiah 10:15-16

Week 3

"Ask me and I will tell you remarkable secrets you do not know about things to come."

Jeremiah 33:3

Week 4

"The human heart is the most deceitful of all things,
and desperately wicked.
Who really knows how bad it is?
But I, the Lord, search all hearts
and examine secret motives.
I give all people their due rewards,
according to what their actions deserve."

Jeremiah 17:9-10

Week 5

This is what the L<small>ORD</small> says:
"Don't let the wise boast in their wisdom,
or the powerful boast in their power,
or the rich boast in their riches.
But those who wish to boast
should boast in this alone:
that they truly know me and understand that I am
the L<small>ORD</small>. . . ."

Jeremiah 9:23-24

Week 6

"For I know the plans I have for you," says the L<small>ORD</small>.
"They are plans for good and not for disaster, to give
you a future and a hope."

Jeremiah 29:11

Meet Our Abingdon Women Authors

Jessica LaGrone is Dean of the Chapel at Asbury Theological Seminary and an acclaimed pastor, teacher, and speaker who enjoys leading retreats and events throughout the United States. She previously served as Pastor of Creative Ministries at The Woodlands UMC in Houston, Texas. She is the author of *Namesake: When God Rewrites Your Story* and *Broken and Blessed: How God Changed the World Through One Imperfect Family*. She and her husband, Jim, have two young children. For speaking and booking information and to follow her blog, Reverend Mother, visit jessicalagrone.com.

Babbie Mason is an award-winning singer and songwriter; a women's conference speaker; a leader of worship celebration-concerts for women; adjunct professor of songwriting at Lee University; and television talk-show host of *Babbie's House*. She has led worship for national and international events hosted by Billy Graham, Charles Stanley, Anne Graham Lotz, Women of Faith, and others. She is the author of *Embraced by God* and *This I Know for Sure*. For information about speaking and events, visit babbie.com.

Kimberly Dunnam Reisman is known for her effective and engaging preaching and teaching. Kim serves as the Executive Director of Next Step Evangelism Ministries and Adjunct Professor at United Theological Seminary. Kim is the author or co-author of numerous books and studies, including *The Christ-Centered Woman: Finding Balance in a World of Extremes*. The mother of three adult children, Kim and her husband live in West Lafayette, Indiana. For information about speaking and events, visit kimberlyreisman.com.

Melissa Spoelstra is a popular women's conference speaker, Bible teacher, and writer who is passionate about helping other women to seek Christ and know Him more intimately through serious Bible study. Melissa is the author of *Jeremiah: Daring to Hope in an Unstable World* and the upcoming 2015 study, *Joseph*. She lives in Dublin, Ohio, with her pastor husband and four kids. For events and booking information and to follow her blog, visit MelissaSpoelstra.com.

Cindi Wood is a sought-after speaker and Bible teacher with events throughout the United States and abroad. Through biblically-based teaching coupled with humor from daily experience, Cindi offers hope and encouragement to women of all ages and walks of life. She is the author of numerous books and Bible studies, including *Anonymous: Discovering the Somebody You Are to God* and the Frazzled Female Series. Cindi lives in Kings Mountain, North Carolina with her husband, Larry. For events and booking information, visit FrazzledFemale.com.

Learn more at AbingdonWomen.com.

More Abingdon Women Bible Studies

Namesake
Explore the transformational power of God through biblical characters who met God and whose lives and names were changed forever. As you meet Abraham and Sarah, Jacob, and more, you will discover that God wants to be just as intimately involved in your story.
978-1-4267-7804-9

Broken and Blessed
Traces the story of the Genesis family from Adam and Eve to Joseph and uncovers how God brings blessing from brokenness. This study allows us to explore how God can use our own imperfect families to bring blessing in a hurting and broken world.
978-1-4267-7841-4

Embraced by God
Every woman longs to know she is loved, accepted, and valued. Drawing upon her own personal journey as God's beloved daughter, contemporary gospel singer Babbie Mason equips women to accept God's unfailing love.
978-1-4267-7794-3

This I Know For Sure
Examine your personal relationship with God, make up your mind to believe God's Word, regardless of your feelings or circumstances, and take hold of some non-negotiable principles of the faith.
978-1-4267-7569-7

The Christ-Centered Woman
Help women discover balance at every age and stage of life by confronting the daily chaos of competing demands from a new perspective. Explore what the Bible teaches about Christ-centered living.
978-1-4267-7568-0

Anonymous
Helps women discover their uniqueness and significance to Christ by exploring some of the "anonymous" women of the Bible. Though we do not know their names, they all were known and loved by God.
978-1-4267-9218-2

Kit Box available on all Abingdon Women's studies.
Contents include one each of the following: participant book, leader guide, DVD, and a preview book. Each piece can also be purchased individually.

Learn more at AbingdonWomen.com.